THE LIFE OF GOD

IN THE

SOUL OF MAN

IN MODERN ENGLISH

By Henry Scougal 1650-1678

Updated English by Paul Lamb

Dedication

This modernized version of Scougal's book is dedicated to all who struggle with the discrepancies between the teachings and practices of organized religion and the word of God. Jesus told us that His true followers abide in His word, and in doing so, will come to know the truth and be set free from sin. He said He will set them free indeed (John 8:31-38). He told us that His Spirit will guide us into all the truth (John 16:13). Today, if you hear His voice, do not harden your heart. Surrender completely to God and join in with all who have learned to give God all the glory for all the great things He has done!

This is also dedicated to the small remnant of true believers out there. The things you write, say, and sing testify to the life of God in your souls and the spiritual discernment that only the Holy Spirit can give. May God pour out His Spirit upon you beyond all you could ever think or imagine! As Whitefield had wished, oh that the kingdom of God would come with great power once again!

Seek the LORD and his strength; seek his presence continually!

1 Chronicles 16:11 ESV

You have said, "Seek my face." My heart says to you, "Your face, LORD, do I seek."

Psalm 27:8 ESV

I will return again to my place, until they acknowledge their guilt and seek my face, and in their distress earnestly seek me.

Hosea 5:15 ESV

All these things my hand has made, and so all these things came to be, declares the LORD. But this is the one to whom I will look: he who is humble and contrite in spirit and trembles at my word.

Isaiah 66:2 ESV

What agreement has the temple of God with idols? For we are the temple of the living God; as God said, "I will make my dwelling among them and walk among them, and I will be their God, and they shall be my people. Therefore go out from them, says the Lord, and touch no unclean thing; and I will be a father to you, and you shall be sons and daughters to me, says the Lord Almighty." Since we have these promises, beloved, let us cleanse ourselves from every defilement of body and spirit, bringing holiness to completion in the fear of God.

2 Corinthians 6:16-7:1 ESV

But I am afraid that as the serpent deceived Eve by his cunning, your thoughts will be led astray from a sincere and pure devotion to Christ.

2 Corinthians 11:3 ESV

Or do you not know that the unrighteous will not inherit the kingdom of God? Do not be deceived: neither the sexually immoral, nor idolaters, nor adulterers, nor men who practice homosexuality, nor thieves, nor the greedy, nor drunkards, nor revilers, nor swindlers will inherit the kingdom of God. And such were some of you. But you were washed, you were sanctified, you were justified in the name of the Lord Jesus Christ and by the Spirit of our God.

1 Corinthians 6:9-11 ESV

It is the Spirit who gives life; the flesh is no help at all. The words that I have spoken to you are spirit and life.

John 6:63 ESV

Contents

Part One

Part Two

Part Three

Prologue

BY PAUL LAMB

P rior to the Great Awakening, the now famous hymn writer, Charles Wesley, gave a copy of Scougal's book to George Whitefield. The rest is history. No other period in history has been accompanied by so much power to bring conviction of man's sinfulness, unworthiness, and the subsequent radical life changing infusion of the life of God into the souls of men.

Whitefield was literally killing himself as he tried to address the conviction of his sinfulness and unworthiness through his human efforts in the exercise of Christianity as a religion. He had more faith than today's churchgoers, but God wanted him to have the real thing. Like Martin Luther, all his studies as he pursued a career in ministry, and all his excessive discipline and self-denial brought him no relief. Also like Luther, by the grace and power of God, he was released from his vain religion that had a form of godliness, yet lacked the power of God. It is this power that brings true conversion, freedom from sin, intimacy with God, deep assurance, and most importantly, the sincere and pure devotion to Christ that true believers are called to preserve against the devil's schemes. The Spirit of God had conceived the life of God in his soul.

The difference between the lives of those who were awakened by the power of God back then and those who are "converted" into churchgoers today is like the difference between night and day. Unfortunately, few know the difference, and leadership in organized religion wants to keep the control, authority, and position it has.

The testimonies of those who found the real thing during the great revivals include those of many pastors and elders who had previously prided themselves for holding what they thought was the true gospel and sound doctrine. They thought they had true conversion, the indwelling Spirit, justification, and Christ in their hearts already. But when the Spirit of God came upon them with full conviction and the power of the new birth, they became born again in truth. Now they were able to realize the difference, because now they had personally experienced both.

This is the story of Church history repeated over and over. A real move of God is replaced by the energies and wisdom of man, resulting in the decline of true conversions. This is followed by God's mercy as he awakens a new generation, only to have man take charge with the machinery of organized religion once again.

If we take George Whitefield's words and put them in

modern English, his quote can convey the significance and strength it originally possessed.

"I didn't know what real Christianity was until God sent me this excellent book."

The churches of our generation are just as lifeless and powerless as the churches were prior to the Great Awakening. We are content with a phantom new birth, born out of the will of the flesh and the will of man. We have lawlessness, entitlement, worldliness, programs, hype, emotionalism, fleshly mimicking of the Holy Spirit's influences, entertainment, and ear tickling teachings instead of the life of God in our souls, manifesting in Christ-likeness.

We have replaced a sincere and pure devotion to Christ with a devotion to church, church leaders, outward religion, and doctrines that divide. Or even worse, we have replaced the infusion of the life of God in our soul with a false assurance derived from our praying some prayer in a fleshly attempt to get fire insurance or to comply with the religious teachings we received. This is usually done without the Spirit's conviction, influence, or power to bring a new birth. And then we believe we have already settled the issue as we resist the conviction of the Spirit by putting our faith in "Once saved, always saved."

In the dance of life, God leads and we follow. He leads by calling us by name. We hear and recognize our Shepherd's voice, so we follow Him. He continues to lead as He takes up residence in our souls, giving us a hunger for His presence, His word, and holiness. Because He first loved us, we follow with a deep love for Him that governs all our behavior. We now know by experience what Jesus meant when He said that those who love Him keep His commandments. God says that those who are led by His Spirit are the sons of God.

In the dance of organized religion, men and women lead and create doctrine. And then they ask God to bless their plans and ministries. In organized religion, people choose when and how they are "saved" and what conditions God is supposed to agree to.

Those with merely external religion struggle to wear their outward form of religion that never seems quite comfortable. It is because they are still in the flesh. Just like a child wearing a superman costume on Halloween is still a child, they are still the old man. Then they remain in the driver's seat of their life as if this supposed conversion has completely satisfied God's will. Before long, they drift back into the world, even though they may continue to go to church.

Judge this situation for yourself. Which dance is true to the nature and character of God? Who shepherds who? Will the Creator submit to the will of His rebellious and arrogant creatures?

Do not be deceived, the unrighteous will not inherit the kingdom of God (1 Corinthians 6:9-11). Those who practice lawlessness will be cast away with no reward for their church services. Not because they didn't have faith in grace, but because lawlessness is the damning evidence of a false conversion (Matthew 7:21-24).Those who are saved by grace through faith have the seed of God in them and can no longer practice lawlessness (1 John 3:3-10). Those who claim to have this seed, the down payment of their salvation, but don't have the real thing, are being deceived.

May God raise up a new generation of true believers that are served by men who have the real thing, are led by the Spirit, reject the shallow surface religion of modern Christianity, and protect their sincere and pure devotion to Christ against the schemes of the devil.

May 2016

Acknowledgment

All of the credit and glory goes to our Triune God. He initiated the original work in the 1600's and this modern English version. He has energized, inspired, directed, and instructed all along the way. His will be done, His kingdom come!

Preface

BY GILBERT BURNET

This age groans under a massive overload of new Christian books. Although the many recently published that are good balance the great swarm of unhealthy or useless ones, everyone complains of the unnecessary burden and hassle all these new books unleash on us. The truth is that printing has become a trade. The presses must keep churning out books, even if they are nothing but trash. This keeps the business going and the work force working.

We have seen a lot of excellent books on devotion and holy living lately in our own language. Maybe no period in history in any language can compare to today in this regard. These books express true Christianity without doctrinal errors and biases, and have been purged of the false representations of Christianity that are common today. Some of these misrepresentations are that Christianity consists in either external performances, in mechanical hearts following the current popular forms of Christianity, or in following the latest popular opinions and topics.

This current bountiful supply of excellent books is clearly a design to make us like God in both our inward state of mind and in our everyday attitudes, speech, and actions. It was for this end that Christ walked the earth and died for us. He taught this and modeled this when He walked among us.

Christ died to take away sin - not only, or even most importantly, to secure our pardon. Our pardon, this offer of peace with God, was only the start of God's purpose in the cross. He died in order to make provisions for a greater end result. The plan of Christ's death was to make it possible that all mankind would be encouraged to enter into a life of holy obedience. This design of the cross also brings all the spiritual blessings, the hopes of eternal happiness, and the fears of eternal miseries into our view. Both the life and death of Christ provide the clearest depiction of God's standards, with a pure and undefiled example for all to follow. The message of the cross can also make everyone confident that He will supply His grace to support and strengthen our efforts toward living in holy obedience, as well as His unerring providence directing everything that concerns us.

The appropriateness and true excellence of every teaching of true Christianity that are far above what is understood because they come from the authority of the Law-giver, have been fully expounded as well. The truth revealed in all that has been created, and in the revelation of God in Scripture was never expressed more fully or clearly since the Apostolic Age than it has now. The mouths of all those who use intimidation to push their opinions and agendas are stopped, and the secret doubts of more inquisitive minds have been silenced.

This serious subject has been handled with all the proper decencies of unforced wit and good language, for we live in a day when this is our custom. Therefore, this subject has not been embellished with artificial and forced strains of wit and eloquence. We would rather have it objected to out of ignorance than to have it artificially inflated by such tactics.

But in spite of all this, when we consider the age in which we live, we must be moved to pour out a flood of grief and lamentation. For few believe or give serious thought to these great truths. It is as if there was some sort of conspiracy against God and Christianity. How is it that the vast majorities of the people unstrap and throw off the light and easy yoke of Christ in order to become enslaved to many corrupt and hurtful lusts and passions? And then they are not satisfied with being as bad as they can be, but desire that the entire world views them that way as they boast in their evil deeds. They even bring more guilt upon themselves by becoming servants of the devil by learning how to corrupt everyone they can.

This horrible condition must deeply affect all who truly love God and all who have a tender compassion for the souls of men. This will, without exception, move all godly people to constant secret mourning and wrestling with God in prayer to avert the heavy judgements that seem to hang over our heads, and that He may turn the hearts of the obstinate and disobedient to the wisdom of the just.

Until God arises and blesses His gospel with more of this success, there is one thing that is second to none for convincing the world of the truth and excellence of our most holy faith. It is when those who profess and embrace our faith walk in all the strictness of a most holy, innocent, and exemplary life. This requires that they avoid hypocrisy (including acting sad and gloomy to convey piety), as well as the frivolities of ungodliness, wickedness, and foolishness, and hold the middle ground of sincere behavior.

This is the only argument that is lacking for convincing the world of the truth of real Christianity. Everyone is more powerfully affected by living examples that they can see than they are by lectures or reasoning, regardless of how strong or convincing they are. It is easier to recognize the truth in another's life, and this leaves a deeper impression than persuasive arguments. The lectures on the truths and evidences for the validity of true Christianity don't have much impact on us until we have given them serious and frequent consideration. Only then we may be satisfied regarding their validity.

When we hear someone who is a good communicator, we are not sure if that speaker really believes what has been said. We tend to suspect that the speaker is showing wit or eloquence at our expense. And we think that we are being persuaded to adopt opinions that will profit the speaker in some way.

But when we see people pursuing a constant course of holiness when this course causes great pain or loss and doesn't cater to their worldly wellbeing, we have good reason to believe they really do believe the truths that oblige them to live this way.

Since the attesting miracles of the early church, nothing has had a greater impact on the world than the exemplary lives and painful martyrdoms of the real Christians. These things made people of all walks of life look with amazement at the teachings that worked so powerfully on people of every class and culture. They marveled as they witnessed the poorly educated, the lower classes of society, the women and children all rise to do and suffer beyond what their greatest heroes and most celebrated philosophers had ever done.

In the days of the martyrs, the defenders of the Christian faith pointed to the lives of the Christians to prove that their doctrine was holy. They concluded that there could be nothing but good in these teachings that resulted in such amazing lives for all who followed them.

Unfortunately, we must point to the lives of people who pretend to be Christians, and who pretend to follow the commandments and teachings of our most holy faith when we write such defenses of the faith today. Therefore, we can no longer use the lives of professing Christians as proof for the validity of the Christian faith. Yes, by God's grace there are still some beautiful and shining examples of real Christianity among us. But how truly few there are and how hard they are to find in the midst of such a large number of professing Christians who are nothing.

Those without moral restraint and the rebellious are hardened against Christianity and have raised two main objections to discredit it. The first objection is that they do not see those who profess Christianity living like they really take their faith seriously. I have heard them say that if Christians believed that the great God governed all human affairs, knows all we do, will call us all to account for it, and will reward or punish us accordingly in an endless and unchangeable state, they could not live the way most professing Christians do. If they truly believed these things, they would not hesitate to renounce all the vain pursuits and follies of this world, and give themselves up completely to a holy and exact course of life.

The second argument against Christianity is directed toward those in whom they cannot find visible faults in their character. They claim that they have reason to believe that those who do live lives that appear quite blameless are only doing so in order to cover some hidden agenda that will become apparent when the right opportunity presents itself. They conclude that these people are secretly as bad as the rest, only disguising it by the external appearance. Or that everything they do is a result of their ability to control their actions in order to accomplish some secret plan or another.

When those who are hardened against Christianity cannot use either of these arguments to discredit everyone, in spite of their natural inclination to either find or make up something in order to find fault, their final judgment is that these people are gloomy and sullen. They accuse them of getting pleasure from their sour dignity of manner through their control over their bodies or through their indoctrination. They claim that this satisfaction is just like the satisfaction that others get from their immoral and extravagant follies.

These arguments against our faith, especially the first one, must be argued using real evidences that refute them. The strict conduct of our lives and our extremely serious and fervent devotions must demonstrate that we are controlled by a strong belief in the authority of that law which governs our every action. Simply abstaining from gross immoralities will not be an adequate counterargument, because those who try to live decent lives without Christianity do the same. Unfortunately this too has become rare, as fools usually mock at the concept of shame and the understanding of sin. These mockers consider these things to be evidences of discontentment derived from a strict and thorough Christian indoctrination.

In order to counter these arguments, we must abstain from all things that are below the dignity of a real Christian and that strengthen a corrupt generation in their vices. What does endless gaming indicate, especially when accompanied by so much greed and passion as is the custom of people today? It is an indication that people do not know how to spend their time. Therefore, they play it away idly at best.

What can we say about the constant crowds at the theaters, "Especially when the stage is so defiled with atheism and all sorts of immorality?" This, too, demonstrates that people do not know how to fill up so many hours of the day. Therefore, this evil device must fill the void to waste these hours away. Those who waste their time this way fill their eyes and ears with sensory images that corrupt their minds, or at least fill their imaginations with very unpleasant and hurtful images. We already have more than enough corruption brewing in us, ready to spring up in our hearts and minds. As if this isn't bad enough, we cultivate and improve this corruption with the arts.

What about the constant socializing for the majority of one's waking hours? How trifling at best and how hurtful are the bulk of these conversations? Let those who are engaged in this behavior declare the truth of the matter.

How much time is spent in the vanities of dressing, applying makeup, and other similar activities? These things corrupt everyone by feeding the vanity of those who spend their time this way, and by stirring up lusts in others who are exposed to the sight of this vanity.

All these things that strengthen this corrupt generation in their vices are observed in the lives of many who desire to be recognized as good Christians, who are regular attenders of church, and who often partake of communion. It is no wonder that the ungodly conclude that these professing Christians do not really believe that everyone will be held accountable for all they do. It doesn't take much intelligence to realize that the lives of these people who want to pass as Christians do not agree with the teachings of Christianity. If they believed they were accountable for everything they did, they would not behave the way they do. Some failures now and then don't justify this conclusion. But a habit and lifestyle of these behaviors is an argument against that kind of religion, and is one that cannot be answered.

After we have escaped these things that are beneath the dignity of our faith, we must realize that this is only part of our proper course in life. It is not enough that we abstain from all that is not compatible with the nature of Christ. We must be doing that which is good and acceptable, expressing this new nature in every instance as our position in life and circumstances dictate. We are to do good to all, forgive injuries, comfort all in trouble, and supply the needs of the poor. But more importantly, we are to study how to move the souls of all people into the abundant life Christ offers. We must improve upon what influences we may have with anyone to this end, raising them to the awareness and understanding of God and of another life. The most effective way that which provides the most impact upon the hearts and minds of those who hear, is by living a consistent, genuine, and most holy life.

And for the other arguments against our faith, there is no wall or protection from the suspicions of the cynical. Even so, we must be careful to avoid everything that could arouse them. Any secret interactions with people of questionable character, any bizarre behavior that is lawful that might defame someone, draw criticisms toward us, or create gossip about us, should all be avoided. To sum it up, we should not do or say anything that is forced, unnatural, or not genuine.

No matter what one thinks, actions that are premeditated and do not flow effortlessly, will not be accepted as genuine and sincere. The actions that are forced in such a way will appear repulsive and hypocritical to others. They will provide the ungodly with reasons to be suspicious of our intentions and to lose respect for our faith, especially to those who are already watching with a critical attitude towards Christianity.

If there were more Christians who lived genuine,

sincere lives without any pretense, the atheists would be more convinced of the reality of our faith, or at least more ashamed, and their lack of confidence would be seen on their faces. This would impact them far more than the best attempts at proving the truth of our faith in carefully researched writings and well-prepared sermons. This would be especially true if more professing Christians demonstrated a spirit of love toward all and goodness. Christians must set aside the factions and animosities among themselves that weaken the holiness of their inner man, expose them to the ridicule of their adversaries, and make them easy prey for everyone who stands against Christianity.

There is hardly anything imaginable that is more of an inexcusable contradiction than when people who profess a religion that has one great theme of mutual love, tolerance, gentleness of spirit, and compassion to all people manifest the fruit of their factions and animosities in ungodly behavior. Christianity is supposed to be characterized by the agreement on the essential parts of Christian doctrine, while differing only in some less solid and more disputable points. When professing Christians maintain these differences with a passion way beyond their significance, using all imaginable excesses of force when they can, or at least all bitterness of spirit, it contradicts their claims to be followers of Christ. Every impartial observer can only be astonished by such actions. They can argue convincingly that this

Christianity that professes love but manifests all the acts of hatred is full of contradictions.

But the deep convictions I have for these things have carried me away. The goal of this preface was to simply introduce the following book. It was written by a godly and highly educated fellow Englishman. He wrote it for the private use of a highly respected friend of his without any intentions of having it published. But when others saw it, they were struck by both the excellent intentions it contained and the exceptionally clear and pleasant style. And they observed its unforced and unadulterated systematic way of presentation, and short to the point delivery. They desired that more people could benefit from reading it.

Because I know the author, they asked me to decide if it should be published. My decision came quickly after reading it. Especially because I know firsthand that the author has written only of things he strongly believes and knows intimately. It is a transcript of the divine impressions upon his heart. Therefore, I hope that its sincere and unforced genuineness will both greatly delight and deeply enrich the reader.

I know that the truths in this book have been regularly proclaimed with the great advantages of reason, wit, and eloquence. But the more who bear witness to these divine truths with their lives and words, the more evidence there is to the truth of them. That is why the author, when he saw a letter written by a friend of his to a person of great honor, regarding the rise and progress of a spiritual life, desired both works to be published together. In this other work there were many points that were not in his, as well as many that were. Because the harmony of the two works was so great, he believed that they would strengthen each other when published at the same time.

The author urged his friend to publish his letter, but he would not until the author agreed to publish his also. Therefore, the reader has both of these works in one book. These letters should be read carefully, having the same seriousness that the authors had in writing them. Those who examine them in this way will not be sorry for putting forth so much effort.

G. Burnet

Notes to the Modern Reader

This modern English version does not include the second book (*Rules and Instructions for a Holy Life*).

Words like inveigle, sedulous, lineaments, flagitious, and adumbrate were replaced. Words and phrases with meanings that have changed or have been obscured due to the passing of time have been updated.

God used the original version to convert many of the chosen instruments He used during the Great Awakening. Since then, He has used it to lead many more out of the outward, empty religion of organized Christianity, and to encourage and edify those who have received the real thing. Pray that God will do similar works in our generation. Grace and peace be given to you through Jesus.

THE LIFE OF GOD
IN THE
SOUL OF MAN
IN MODERN ENGLISH

By Henry Scougal

Updated English by Paul Lamb

Part One

The Reason This is Written

Because you are my dear friend, you are sure to get all of my efforts to address your curiosity about true godliness. Your interest in true Christianity is an appropriate match with my occupation. Therefore, I will not have to go out of my way in order to provide you with this information and will not delay in fulfilling my debt of friendship. The advancement of moral excellence and holiness is the single duty of my profession, and I hope you make it your primary subject of study. That makes this the perfect situation for me to express my friendship and gratitude. I will not delay any longer. I will fulfill my promise to you regarding these things.

I know that you have access to better sources of this information and that nothing I write will be new to you. Even so, I am hopeful that you will accept what I write because it comes from one you choose to honor as a friend, and because it is written with you in mind. Hopefully God will direct my thoughts so that you will find something useful in what I write.

I am confident that you won't mind if I begin with the

basics in order to provide a more useful organization for this essay. By starting with the nature and properties of real Christianity, I will lay an elementary foundation. In this way, I will be able to fully express my thoughts as I work to complete this essay. This will result in my writing many things to you that, because of your knowledge of these things, would otherwise be unnecessary.

Mistakes About Christianity

I cannot speak of Christianity without great sorrow and grief, because out of the many who claim to be Christians, so few understand what it means to be a Christian. Some believe that Christianity is a matter of understanding, of accurate doctrine, and of opinions. All they can say about their faith is that they believe one of the different opinions, and have joined one of the many denominations that Christianity has so sadly been divided into.

Others believe that Christianity is a matter of one's actions, in a constant course of external duties or in the performance of certain standards. If they live in peace with their neighbors, exercise self-control in eating and drinking, give money regularly, attend church services, pray, and occasionally give to the needy, they think that they have done all that is required.

There are others who put all of their Christianity in

their feelings, in emotional experiences, and in their ecstasy in devotion. All they pursue is to pray passionately, to think of heaven with pleasure, and to experience warm feelings when they seek their Savior's affections. Based on these things, they convince themselves that they are deeply in love with Him. They assume that they are truly saved because of their experiences. They consider this feeling-based confidence to be the greatest of Christian blessings.

All these ideas about Christianity are not accurate representations of the straight and narrow path that leads to life. At best, they are only ways to obtain the real thing or simply practices of it. These things are frequently mistaken to be the whole of Christianity.

Even wickedness and improper behaviors are sometimes claimed to be religious activities. I am not referring to the very sinful practices of the non-Christians as they worship their gods. There are way too many professing Christians who justify their character flaws and call their corrupt affections holy, whose hurtful character and gloomy pride are called strict Christian behavior. Their fierce anger and bitter rage against their enemies is excused as holy zeal. And their unreasonable irritability with those in authority or rebellion against civil authority is justified as Christian courage and conviction.

What Real Christianity Is

But real Christianity is considerably different, and those who know it think in totally different ways. They despise all those shadows of Christianity and false imitations of it. They know by experience that true Christianity is a union of the soul with God. It is a real impartation of the divine nature. It is the image of God sketched on the soul. In the words of the apostle, "it is Christ formed within us." In its most complete, precise, and brief definition, it is a divine life in us. I know of no better way to describe it. Therefore, I will use these terms as I write this essay. I will show why it is first called a life, and then why it is divine.

Its Permanency and Stability

I choose to call real Christianity a life primarily because of its permanency and stability. Real Christianity does not suddenly spring to life only to fade away. Nor is it a passion of the mind that may rise to the heights of ecstasy and appear to move someone to perform extraordinary feats. Most people have a strong belief that they must do something to obtain the salvation of their souls. This may motivate them with considerable urgency. But in a short time they grow weary and quit. They were only fired up, but now they are not. They sprang up fresh and tall, but they withered quickly. It is because they had no root within themselves. These sudden periods of vigorous activity are like the violent and convulsive movements of a body right after the head is cut off. All of these violent and sudden energetic motions cannot last very long.

In contrast to this, the actions of holy souls are consistent and regular. These actions come from a source that is permanent and full of life. It is true that this divine life doesn't always continue with the same amount of strength and vigor. And yes, it sometimes suffers times of weakness when holy men find it more difficult to resist temptations. There may be periods with less excitement in the performance of their duties. Yet even during these times, the divine life is not fully extinguished, nor are they abandoned to the power of the selfish desires that influence and control the rest of the world.

Its Freedom and Unforced Behavior

Again, true Christianity can be called a life because it is an indwelling, unrestrained, and energizing source. Those who make progress in this life are moved to action by more than external motivations. They are not driven merely by threats, bribed with promises, or constrained by laws; but they are powerfully inclined to what is good, and delight in doing it. The love that a godly man has for God and for doing good comes primarily from his new nature instructing and prompting him, instead of from commands. He doesn't live this life of devotion because of mandatory obligations to appease God's justice or to sooth a guilty conscience.

Instead, these religious exercises are the genuine manifestations of the divine life. They are the natural activities of the new-born soul. He prays, gives thanks, and repents not merely because they are commanded. He does these things because he is aware of his needs, the goodness of God, and the foolishness and misery of a sinful life. His generosity is not forced, nor are his gifts to the poor extorted from him, for his love makes him desire to give. And even if there were no instructions to do these things, his "heart would create a generous course in life." Injustice, lack of self-control, and all other character defects are as contrary to his nature and character as the lowest of actions are to the most civilized. They are as foreign to him as shameful behaviors and filthy speech are to those who are naturally modest. Therefore, I echo the words of the apostle John, "No one born of God makes a practice of sinning, for God's seed abides in him, and he cannot keep on sinning because he has been born of God."

Although holy and godly people regularly view the law of God and have a great regard for it, it is its reasonableness, purity, and goodness more than the penalties of the law that influence them. They consider it excellent and desirable, and that there is great reward for keeping it. The divine love that moves them causes them to be a law to themselves. "Who shall prescribe a law to those who love? Love is a more powerful law which moves them to action."

The words of our blessed Savior, to some degree, are

true of His followers too. He said that doing the Father's will was His food. Our natural appetite is enough to ensure that we eat meals regularly. Therefore, we don't have to give any thought to how necessary it is to eat. In the same way, those who possess the divine life are moved by a natural and unforced inclination to do that which is good and commendable without having to consider its importance.

External motivations are often very helpful for exciting and stirring up this inner source of life, especially when this new life has just begun or is in a weakened state. In these conditions, it is often so weak that a man is hardly even aware of its existence. He finds it difficult to take even one step forward in this life. But this is overcome when he is urged forward by his hopes, fears, and the pressure of some hardship; a clear instance of God's mercy; the authority of God's word; or the encouragement of others.

If a person in such a weakened state is conscientious and consistent in his obedience, is sincerely groaning under the awareness of his condition, and desires to perform his duties with more enthusiasm and strength, the divine life is beginning to take root. Although it is weak and not very bright, it will certainly be cherished by the influences of heaven and will grow to greater maturity.

In contrast, there are those who completely lack this inner source of life and have no desire for it. They are content with the performances prompted by their religious indoctrination or custom, the fear of hell, or worldly notions of heaven. Such people are not real Christians any more than a puppet can be called a real man. This forced and artificial religion is typically burdensome and lifeless. It is like lifting a heavy weight. It is cold and heartless, like the uneasy compliance of a wife married against her will, who endures out of some sense of virtue or honor, instead of out of love for her husband.

Therefore, this lifeless religion is also incomplete and unwilling to go the extra mile. This is especially true when it comes to duties that require one to deny the carnal nature. Those enslaved to this type of religion will not do any more than what is absolutely required in their minds. They are compelled by law and they hate going beyond what it demands of them. You can be sure that they will embrace any rationalization in order to do only the bare minimum.

In contrast, those who have real Christianity hold nothing back from God and are not enslaved to the carnal nature. Complaints about the duties of godliness are foreign to them. So is the "that's asking too much" thinking of the false forms of Christianity. Those who have given themselves completely to God will never think they do too much for Him.

True Christianity is a Divine Source

So I hope that you can see that there are many very good reasons for calling true Christianity a life or vital inner source. I also hope you can see how important it is to distinguish it from religious obedience that is forced and depends on external motivations.

Now I will demonstrate why I call it a divine life. It is accurately called a divine life. Not only because of its source and pattern from which it takes its form. Not only because God is the author of it. Not only because it is the Holy Spirit's power that works in the souls of men. Beyond all these reasons, it is a divine life because of its very nature. It is the pattern of divine perfections and the image of the Almighty shining from the souls of men. It is a real sharing of His nature. It is a beam of the eternal light, and a drop of the infinite ocean of His goodness. It is truly stated that those who possess this life have "God dwelling in their souls" and "Christ formed in them."

What the Natural Life Is

Before I go deeper into the details of the divine life that is true Christianity, it makes sense to define the natural life of those who don't know the divine life. This natural life, or animal life, rules the lives of those who don't have the divine life. My understanding of this natural life is that it is simply our inclinations and propensity toward the things that are pleasing and acceptable to the physical nature. Or it can be described as self-love springing up and branching out into any and all of man's appetites and inclinations. I consider our senses to be the root and foundation of this animal life. By senses, I mean those that are the opposite of faith. These senses lead to our perceptions and sensations of what things are pleasing to us, and what are unpleasant to us.

In and of themselves, these natural senses are not evil or guilty of wrong. Instead, they are a demonstration of the wisdom of our Creator. They provide His creatures with the necessary appetites that result in the preservation and welfare of their lives. They are given to the animals to accomplish for them what God's written instructions are to accomplish for us. This is how God directs them in order to accomplish His purposes in creating them.

But man was made to accomplish higher purposes. He is to be guided by a greater kind of instruction. God created us for a much higher and nobler purpose. Therefore, when one is guided by the inclinations of the animal life to violate or neglect these higher purposes, he is held responsible and is condemned.

Our physical appetites and inclinations are not to be completely uprooted and destroyed. They are to be moderated and over-ruled by a superior and more excellent source. Therefore, the difference between a true Christian and a wicked man is that the one is primarily directed by the divine life, and the other by the natural life.

The Different Tendencies of the Natural Life

How strange it is to observe all the different paths this natural life can carry those who are governed by it only. This is according to differing circumstances that work together with the natural life to produce these many paths. Without thinking, those who are led by this natural life often make a serious mistake. They think that their souls are not in danger based on the apparent differences between their path and the paths of others. In their minds they are not as worthy of judgment as are those on a different path. They fail to realize that all of these differing paths flow from the very same source.

Consider the natural characteristics and attitudes of the souls of men. We observe that some are frivolous, playful, and carefree, making their behavior extravagant and ridiculous. Others are naturally serious and severe, so that their every action is so dignified that others hold them in high regard and esteem. Some people have a party-pooping, unhappy, and gloomy character, so that they are never happy and can't tolerate those who are.

But not everyone is born with such sour and dissatisfied dispositions. For some have a sweetness and the desire to see others benefited rooted in their character. Such people find the greatest pleasure in the benefits of socializing with others. They enjoy the mutual gratification of friendship, and desire nothing more than to have others obligated to them. It is a good thing that this multifaceted tenderness is provided by the Creator, for it makes up for the world's lack of the true love of God in the hearts of man. In this way, men may still be inclined to do something for one another's good.

When it comes to education, some have never been taught to follow any rules other than those of pleasure or advantage. Others still are so inclined to observe the strictest rules of decency and honesty, and even virtue, that they are barely able to do anything that they believe to be beneath them or to be unworthy.

So we see that there is a vast range in the conduct of mere natural souls. This diversity results from the strength or weakness of their intelligence or discernment, and from the extent that they choose to use them. The lack of self-restraint, lust, injustice, oppression, and all the other ungodliness that abounds in the world and makes it so miserable, are the manifestations of self-love. These are the effects of the animal life when it is neither overpowered by the life of God in the soul, nor governed by natural reason.

But if self-love takes hold of reason, and partners with discernment and intelligence, it will often disdain the more obvious vices. In so doing, one may rise to a reasonable imitation of virtue and goodness. Self-love may be enough to bring restraint, if one has enough reason to consider the damage the lack of self-control and unrestrained lust inflicts on his health, fortune, and reputation. Some observe ethical rules in dealing with others as the best way to be successful and to maintain their credibility in the world.

But this is not the only way that this natural life can be manifested with the help of reason. It can take a higher path that comes close to the appearance of godliness and true Christianity. It may incline a man to diligently study divine truths. And why not, for this can bring as much pleasure and satisfaction to curious and inquisitive minds as can any other subject.

This natural life can make men zealously maintain and spread the opinions they have adopted. They can have a strong desire to have others submit to their way of thinking and to agree with their version of Christianity. Because eloquence is pleasing on any subject, they can take great pleasure in hearing and composing excellent messages about various topics of Christianity.

Beyond all of this, some who only have this natural life can bring themselves to great heights of apparent devotion. The wonderful things said about heaven can make even a natural heart fall in love with it. Heaven is described with many metaphors and symbolic pictures in the Bible such as crowns, scepters, rivers of pleasure, etc. Even though they can't understand and don't desire the spiritual pleasures described and shadowed in these things, they can easily have their imaginations affected by them so that they want to be there.

When these merely natural people come to believe that Christ has purchased these wonderful things for them, they may feel a tenderness and affection for this great source of blessings. They can believe that they are thoroughly enamored with Him, even though they continue to be strangers to the holy nature and Spirit of the blessed Jesus. The part played by this natural life in the ecstatic devotions of some melancholy people has been excellently brought to light in the recent writings of several educated and clear-minded men.

In conclusion, assisted by intelligence and reason, this natural life can prompt one to do anything suitable for making life enjoyable, or making one superior and stand out in the world. Although I do not condemn these things in and of themselves, it is very important that we know and consider these things. Then we can keep our priorities straight and learn not to value ourselves based on our attaining these things. It is also important to keep us from viewing the things that stem from our natural appetites and performances as either proof of or the substance of true Christianity.

The Divine Life Defined

It is now time to return to the consideration of the divine life. It is a "life which is hid with Christ in God." Since it is hidden in God, it doesn't have any glorious show or appearance in the world. To the natural man, it will be perceived as an inferior and unappealing notion.

As the animal life is based in a narrow and confined love that is self-serving, and in one's tendencies toward those things that are pleasing to the flesh; so the divine life stands in a love that extends to all and has no limits, and in the mastery over our fleshly inclinations. This mastery over the flesh keeps us from doing the things that we know are not compatible with a holy and pure life.

The root of the divine life is faith; the main branches are love to God, charity to man, purity, and humility. It has been accurately observed that even though these concepts are common, universally used, and do not sound extraordinary, they have powerful meanings. The tongues of men and angels can pronounce nothing more weighty or excellent.

Faith has the same place in the divine life that sense has in the natural life. It is truly nothing more than a type of sense, or experiential awareness of spiritual things. It extends itself into all divine truths. Because of our fallen nature, it has a special relation to the declarations of God's mercy and desire to reconcile sinners to himself through a mediator. Therefore, it is normally called "faith in Jesus Christ" because he is the focal point of these declarations.

Love to God is a delightful and affectionate sense of God's perfections. It makes the soul resign and sacrifice itself completely to him. It desires above all things to please him, and has its greatest delight in fellowship and communion with him. It is ready to do or suffer anything for his sake or at his pleasure. Though this affection may begin from the favors and mercies of God toward us, as it grows and matures, it transcends these concepts. It becomes rooted in his infinite goodness that is manifested in all the works of creation, and in all that he does.

A soul controlled by this divine love, will be enlarged toward all mankind in a sincere and limitless concern because of the relation they have to God, being his creatures and having something of his image stamped upon them. This is that charity I named as the second branch of religion. Under it, all the parts of justice and all the duties we owe to our neighbor are clearly included. He who truly loves the entire world will be equally concerned about the interests of everyone. Such a person will be so far from wronging or injuring anyone, that he will resent anything suffered by another, as if it happened to himself.

By purity, I mean a proper distractedness from the natural life, and a mastery over its inferior appetites. It is a governing of the mind and character of mind, that causes a man to despise and abstain from all pleasures and delights of sense or impulsive desires, which are sinful in themselves, or that tend to extinguish or lessen our delight in more divine and intellectual pleasures. It also implies a resoluteness to endure all the hardships one may meet with in the performance of his duty to God, so that not only integrity and restraint, but also Christian courage and perseverance may be included in it.

Humility imports a deep sense of our own lowliness, with a hearty and affectionate acknowledgment of our owing all that we are to God's manifold grace. It is always accompanied with a profound submission to the will of God, and a great deadness toward both the glory of the world and the applause of men.

These are the highest attributes that either men or angels are capable of. They are the very foundation of heaven laid in the soul. He who has acquired them doesn't have to pry into the hidden rolls of God's decrees, or search the volumes of heaven to know what is determined about his everlasting condition. Instead, he may find a copy of God's thoughts concerning him written in his own heart. His love towards God may give him assurance of God's favor to him. The birth of the happiness he feels as the powers of his soul are conformed to the nature of God, and his compliance with God's will are a sure sign that his joy in the Lord shall be perfected and continued to all eternity. It is for a good reason that someone said: "I would rather see the genuine impressions of a godlike nature on my own soul, than have a vision from heaven or an angel sent to tell me that my name was enrolled in the book of life."

Real Christianity is Better Understood by Actions Than by Words

When we have said all that we can, the secret mysteries of the new nature and divine life can never be sufficiently expressed. Language and words cannot reveal the heights of these mysteries. Nor can they be truly understood by anyone who has not been given this internal spark and been awakened into the awareness and enjoyment of real spiritual things. "There is a spirit in man, and the inspiration of the Almighty gives this understanding."

The power and life of real Christianity may be better expressed in actions than in words. Actions are more responsive to the life of God in the soul, and give a clearer image of the inward source from which they spring. Therefore, we may get the best measurements of those gracious endowments from the way those who have this new life conduct their lives.

The character of this life is especially revealed to us in the perfect example of the holy life of our blessed Savior. A primary purpose of his incarnation was to teach by his practice what he requires of others. He made his own life an exact illustration of those unparalleled rules which he taught us. Therefore, if ever true goodness was visible to mortal eyes, it was when his presence beautified and illuminated this lower world.

Divine Love Exemplified in Our Savior

That sincere and devout affection with which his blessed soul constantly burned toward his Heavenly Father expressed itself in an entire resignation to his will. It was his very food to do the will and finish the work of the One who sent him.

His Diligence in Doing God's Will

To do his Father's will was the exercise of his childhood and the constant employment of his riper age. He didn't hold back any journey or effort while he was about his Father's business. He found infinite contentment and satisfaction in the performance of it. This is seen when being faint and weary with his journey, he rested himself at Jacob's well and asked the Samaritan woman for water. It was the success of his words with her, and the additions that were made to the kingdom of God that filled his mind with such delight. Doing the will of his Father seemed to have overflowed into his very body, refreshing his spirits. It made him forget his thirst and refuse the food that he had sent his disciples to buy. His bodily weakness did not make him less patient and submissive in suffering the will of God, nor less diligent in doing it.

His Patience in Suffering

He endured the harshest afflictions and the most extreme miseries that were ever inflicted on any mortal without feeling rejection or uttering discontentment. He was very aware of what was happening, wasn't unnaturally indestructible, didn't lack emotions, felt pain just as other men, and knew exactly what he was to suffer in his soul. This is made perfectly clear by the "bloody sweat, agony, and deep sorrow of soul" he expressed as he faced these things. In spite of all this, he submitted completely to the intense fulfillment of the Father's will and willingly accepted it.

Jesus prayed to God that "if it were possible," and as one of the gospels has it, "if he were willing that the cup might be removed." Yet he gently added, "nevertheless, not my will but thine be done." Oh how wonderful and important the expressions found in John 12:27 are! Here he first acknowledged the anguish of his spirit, "Now my soul is troubled." This seemed to produce a hesitance, "and what shall I say." And then he attempted to escape his suffering by praying, "Father, save me from this hour." Immediately after he uttered those words, as if on second thought, he said, "but for this purpose I came into the world."

He then concludes, "Father, glorify thy name." Now we shouldn't perceive this as any instability, or reprehensible weakness in the blessed Jesus. He knew all along what he was to suffer, and very resolutely went through with it. But this shows us the inconceivable weight and pressure that he was about to bear. It was so severe and contrary to one's self-preservation, he could not think of it without terror. Yet considering the will of God and the glory that was to overflow to God as a result, he was not only content, but desirous to suffer it.

His Constant Devotion

Another example of Jesus' love to God was his delight in conversing with him by prayer. It made him retire frequently from the world. With the greatest devotion and pleasure he would spend whole nights in that heavenly exercise. He did this even though he had no sins to confess and few worldly interests to pray for. Sadly, these are the only things that tend to drive us to our devotions. In contrast, we may say his whole life was a kind of prayer, a constant course of communion with God. Even if the sacrifice was not always being offered, the fire was kept alive. Neither was the blessed Jesus ever surprised with that lack of vitality or lukewarm spirit that we frequently have to wrestle with before we can be in the proper state for the exercise of devotion.

His Charity to Men

In the second place, I should speak of his love and charity toward all men. The only way to do this is by noting and commenting on the entire history recorded in the Gospels. This is because very little, if anything, that has been recorded of Jesus' words and actions were not designed by him to benefit others. All his miraculous works were instances of his goodness as well as his power. Therefore, they benefitted both those who received the works as well as the witnesses of these miracles. His charity was not confined to his relatives and acquaintances. Nor was all his kindness directed toward the beloved disciple with whom he had a special friendship. Everyone was his friend who obeyed his holy commands (John 15:14). To him, "whoever did the will of his Father" was the same was to him as "his brother, sister, and mother."

Jesus welcomed everyone who came with honest intentions. He did not deny any request which was for the good of those that asked it. Therefore, what was spoken of that Roman Emperor, whom for his goodness they called "the darling of mankind," was really performed by Jesus. No one departed from him with a heavy countenance, except that youth (Mark 10) who was sorry to hear that entrance to the kingdom of heaven was difficult, in that he could not save his soul and his money too. It definitely troubled our Savior to see that when the young man had what he needed to acquire wisdom, he lacked sufficient desire for it. His honorable request had already procured some kindness for him. We see this in what is written, "And Jesus, beholding him, loved him." Should Jesus create a new way to heaven and alter the nature of reality that makes it impossible for a covetous man to be happy?

And what shall I say about his meekness? Who could encounter the monstrous ingratitude and deception of that villain who betrayed him using no harsher terms than these, "Judas, do you betray the Son of Man with a kiss?" What further evidence could we desire of his fervent and limitless charity, than that he willingly laid down his life even for his most bitter enemies? He even mingled his prayer with his blood, asking the Father that his death might not be held against them, but would be the source of eternal life even for those who sought for and secured his death.

His Purity

The third branch of the divine life is purity. It is a neglect of worldly enjoyments and accommodations, and a resolute enduring of all troubles we encounter in living for God's glory. If anyone was completely dead to all the pleasures of the natural life, surely it was the blessed Jesus. He seldom tasted them when they came in his way, and never stepped out of his way to seek them. Though he allowed others the comforts of wedlock and honored marriage with his presence, yet he chose the severity of a virgin life and never knew the nuptial bed. He supplied the needed wine with a miracle, but would not work one for the relief of his own hunger in the wilderness. So gracious and divine was the restraint of his soul, he allowed others to enjoy the lawful gratifications that he considered good to abstain from. He not only supplied their more extreme and pressing needs, but also their smaller and less important wants.

We often hear of our Savior's sighs, groans, and tears. But we never hear that he laughed, and only once that he rejoiced in spirit. He perfectly displayed the character given him by the prophet of old, saying he was "a man of sorrows" and "acquainted with grief." The troubles and hardships of his life were not a result of his inability to choose to avoid them. No one who has walked the earth has had greater advantages for bringing himself to the highest worldly happiness. He who could bring together such a large number of fish into his disciples' net and collect money from the mouth of a fish to pay to the temple tax, could easily have made himself the richest person in the world. Even without any money, he could have maintained an army powerful enough to have removed Caesar from his throne by feeding thousands with a few loaves and small fishes. Instead, he chose to show how little he esteemed all the enjoyments in this world. He chose to live in so poor and low a condition, that "though the foxes had holes, and the bird of the air had nests, yet the Lord and heir of all things had nowhere to lay his head." He did not frequent the courts of princes, nor seek the acquaintance or company of the rich and famous. But as the reputed son of a carpenter, he had fishermen and similar poor people for his companions, and lived in a way that corresponded to this lower class of people.

His Humility

Without any forethought on my part, the consideration of Jesus' purity leads me to speak of his humility also, the last branch of the divine life. His example of humility is the standard for us, so that we might "learn of him to be meek and lowly in heart." At this time I won't elaborate on the infinite and voluntary descent of the eternal Son of God in his taking our nature. I will only elaborate on our Savior's lowly and humble ways while he was in the world. He had none of those sins and imperfections which may justly humble the best of men. He was so entirely swallowed up with a deep sense of the infinite perfections of God, that being manifested in the form of a man he appeared as nothing in his own eyes. He considered that the eminent perfections that shone in his blessed soul were not his own, but the gifts of God. Therefore, he took no credit for them, but with the deepest humility he renounced all pretenses to them. Therefore, he rejected the common title of good master when addressed to his human nature by one who was apparently ignorant of his divinity. "Why do you call me good, there is none good but God only?" It is as if he had said that the goodness of any created being, which is all you consider me to be, is not worthy to be named or taken notice of. It is God alone who is originally and essentially good.

Jesus never made use of his miraculous power for inferior purposes or to show off. He would not gratify the curiosity of the Jews with a sign from heaven. He didn't produce spectacular omens in the sky. He didn't follow the advice of his countrymen and family, who wanted him to perform all his great works in the eyes of the world to make him famous. But when his love prompted him to come to the aid of those who suffered, his humility often led him to conceal the miracles. But when the glory of God and the purpose for which he came into the world required them to be known, he ascribed the entire honor to his Father saying, "Apart from the Father I can do nothing."

I won't elaborate on all the instances of humility in his conduct towards men, but only mention a few. He withdrew himself when they would have made him a king. He submitted not only to his blessed mother, but to her husband while a youth. He allowed all the indignities and affronts of his rude and malicious enemies. The history of his holy life, recorded by those who walked with him, is full of similar demonstrations of his humility. Clearly, the serious and attentive study of his life is the best way to get a correct standard of humility, and of all the other aspects of true Christianity that I have been endeavoring to describe.

But now I will ease the burden of reading by adding some pauses. Let me include a prayer that might be beneficial to one who had formerly entertained some false notions of Christianity, and is beginning to discover what it really is.

A Prayer

"Infinite and eternal Majesty, author and fountain of being and blessedness, how little do we poor sinful creatures know of you and of the way to serve and please you! We talk of Christianity and falsely lay claim to it. But alas! How few there are that know and consider what it really means! How easily we mistake the attachments and emotions of our nature, and the deeds of self-love for the divine graces which alone can make us acceptable in your sight! I am grieved as I consider how long I have wandered, and have been content with vain shadows and false images of devotion and religion. Yet I must acknowledge and adore your goodness, for you have been pleased to begin to open my eyes and to let me see the real prize to pursue. I rejoice to consider what mighty improvements my new nature is capable of, and what a divine quality of spirit shines in those you are pleased to choose and to draw close to you. I praise you for your infinite mercy, for sending your own Son to dwell among men, and instruct them by his example. And for his giving his laws and a perfect pattern of what men are to be. Oh, that the holy life of the blessed Jesus may always be in my thoughts and before my eyes until I receive a deep sense and imprint of those excellent graces that shone so eminently in him! Let me never cease my efforts, until the new and divine nature prevails in my soul and Christ is formed within me."

Part Two

The Excellence and Advantage of Real Christianity

And now, my dear friend, we have discovered the nature of true Christianity. Before I proceed any further, it is appropriate for us to fix our meditations on its excellence and advantages. By this we may be inspired to a more vigorous and diligent performance of the methods that assist us in abiding in the great joy and happiness found in Christ. But, alas! How can words express the inward satisfactions and the hidden pleasures that cannot be truly understood except by those holy souls who feel them? "A stranger doesn't share in their joys" (Proverbs 14:10).

Holiness is the correct quality, the vigorous and healthy state of the soul. The capabilities of the soul had been weakened and disordered. As a result, it could not exercise its intended functions. It had wearied itself with endless tossing and turning, and was never able to find any rest. When that abnormality is removed, it feels healthy. Now there is a proper harmony in its natural aptitudes and a lively power controls every part. Now the mind can discern what is good, and the will can be loyal to it. One's desires and feelings are no longer tied to the inclinations of the physical senses and the influence of external objects. Instead, they are moved by more divine influences and sense the reality of invisible things.

The Excellence of Loving God

Let us descend to an aspect of true Christianity that touches our daily lives and is one of its main branches. We will now consider the love and affection that unites holy souls to God, and the excellence and happiness that it produces. Love is the powerful and dominant passion that regulates all the aptitudes and inclinations of the soul. Both the perfection and happiness of the soul depend on it.

The worth and excellence of a soul is to be evaluated by the object of its love. He who loves inferior and filthy things becomes base and vile. But a noble and well-placed affection advances and improves the spirit into conformity with the perfections it loves. The characteristics and qualities of the loved objects are regularly on one's mind. In conjunction with this focus, by an unknown force and energy, the images of the objects loved are woven into the fabric of the soul, molding and fashioning it into their own likenesses.

Therefore, we see how easily lovers and friends imitate the people they love. Before they know it, they begin to resemble them, not only in their mannerisms, but also in their voice, gestures, personality, and attitudes.

Therefore, we will certainly take on the virtues and inward beauties of the soul, if God and his glory are really the objects and motivations of our love.

Because everyone we interact with in this world has their flaws and individual makeup, we are always in danger of being tarnished and corrupted by placing our affection on them. Emotion easily blinds our eyes, so that we first accept, and then imitate the things that are not Christ-like in them. The true way to improve and advance our souls is by fixing our love on the divine perfections. In doing this, we may always have them before us and acquire the imprint of them on our souls. "Beholding the glory of the Lord with unveiled face, as in a mirror, we are changed into the same image, with ever increasing glory."

What does the one who fixes his gaze and his love on the Uncreated One with a wholehearted and holy ambition look like? He who has raised his eyes toward uncreated beauty and goodness, and has fixed his affection there is of a very different spirit. He has a more excellent and heroic character than the rest of the world. He will have an infinite disdain for all inferior and unworthy things. He will not entertain any low or inferior thoughts which might degrade his high and noble efforts to establish his claim to Christ.

Love is the greatest and most excellent thing we can control. Therefore, giving it to inferior objects is foolishness and self-degradation. It is truly the only thing we can call our own. Other things may be taken from us by violence. But no one can destroy our love. Other things may be considered ours, but by giving our love we give all. To the extent that we transfer the title of our hearts and wills, through which we control our other enjoyments, we give our love.

It is not possible to refuse anything to the one we have given ourselves to by love. It is the privilege of gifts to receive their value from the mind of the giver, and the desire of the giver's heart instead of the outcome of the desire. It may be said that he who loves, not only gives all that he has, but everything that may make the beloved person happy. He would do this because he whole-heartedly seeks the happiness of the beloved, and would really give them if they were in his power to give them. It is from this understanding of what it means to love God that it was said, "In some ways, love for God gives God to himself by the satisfaction it takes in the happiness and perfection of his character." Even though this expression seems to be overreaching, love is truly the most valuable present we can offer to God. Therefore, it is extremely debased when we give it anywhere else.

When love is misplaced, it is frequently expressed in ways that point to its genuine and proper object. These expressions are an indirect way of revealing the proper object of our love. The flattering and blasphemous terms of adoration that men often use to express their love, are the language of the affection that was made and designed for God. The way many are accustomed to speak to great people, though it may be unintentional, speaks an aggressive challenge to the One those titles should be given to. The passion that glorifies its object as Deity should only be given to the One who really is. The unlimited submissions, which would debase the soul if directed to any other, will exalt and ennoble it when placed here. These chains and cords of love are infinitely more glorious than liberty itself. This slavery is nobler than all the empires in the world.

The Advantages of Loving God

Just as loving God advances and elevates the soul; it alone can make it truly happy. The highest and most ravishing pleasures, the most solid and substantial delights that human nature is capable of, are the ones that arise from the affectionate acts of a well-placed and successful love. What embitters love and usually makes it a very troublesome and painful passion is placing it on someone other than God. Some are not worthy enough to deserve it. Others lack the affections and gratitude to return it. Their absence may deprive us of the pleasure of their company, or their sufferings cause us grief. Those who place their primary and highest affection on creatures like themselves are exposed to all these evils. But loving God in the way we were created to delivers us from all of these things.

The Worth of the Object

Love is certainly miserable, full of trouble, and unsettled when its object is not worthy and excellent enough to satisfy the vastness of its capacity. Such an eager and volatile passion will cause emotional stress, and torment the spirit when it finds that its cravings are not satisfied. It is truly so large and limitless in its nature, that it is extremely constricted and confined when limited to anyone other than God. Nothing less than an infinite good can provide room for love to stretch and exert its vitality and activity. Can a little skin-deep beauty or some small degree of goodness match or satisfy a passion that was made for God, and designed to embrace an infinite God?

It is no wonder that lovers can't tolerate rivals and do not want others to love their lover in the way that they do. They know the scantiness and narrowness of the good that they love, that it cannot satisfy two, being in effect too little for one. Therefore love "which is strong as death" breeds "jealousy which is as cruel as the grave." Its coals are coals of fire with a very violent flame.

But love for God doesn't have any mixture of this bitterness. After the soul is fixed on the supreme and all-sufficient good, it finds so much perfection and goodness that not only answers and satisfies its affection, but masters and overpowers it too. It finds all its love to be too faint and sluggish for such a noble object. Its only regret is that it can't command any more. It wishes for the flames of a seraph, and longs for the time when it shall be melted and dissolved completely into love. Because it can do very little by itself, it desires the assistance of the whole creation. It wishes that angels and men would act together with it in the admiration and love of those infinite perfections.

The Certainty of Returned Love

Again, love is accompanied with trouble, when it misses a suitable return of affection. Love is the most valuable thing we can give. By giving it, we effectively give all that we have. Therefore, it is severely distressful to find such a great a gift despised, and that the present that was made of his whole heart doesn't result in any return. Perfect love is a kind of self-dereliction, a wandering out of ourselves. It is a kind of voluntary death, where the lover dies to himself and all his own interests. He is no longer thinking of or caring for his own interests anymore, and is only thinking of how he may please and gratify the one he loves. As a result, he is quite undone, unless he meets with reciprocal affection. He has neglected himself and the other has no regard for him.

But if he is loved in return, he is revived and lives in the soul and care of the person whom he loves. Now he begins to think of his own interests, not because they are his, but because the beloved is pleased to own an interest in them. He becomes dear to himself because he is dear to the other.

But why should I write more regarding something so obvious? Nothing can be clearer than that the happiness of love depends on the return it sees. Here is where the lover of God has an advantage that is beyond what we can say or think. He has placed his affection on the One whose nature is love. The One whose goodness is as infinite as his being, and whose mercy preceded us when we were his enemies. Therefore God will certainly embrace us when we become his friends. It is utterly impossible for God to deny his love to a soul wholly devoted to him, who desires nothing more than to serve and please him. He cannot disdain his own image or the heart in which it is engraved. Love is all the tribute that we can pay him, and it is the sacrifice that he will not despise.

The Presence of the Beloved Person

Another thing which disturbs the pleasure of love, and renders it a miserable and troubled passion, is the absence of and separation from those we love. It is not without a perceptible affliction that friends are apart, even for a short time. It causes sadness to be deprived of the companionship that is so delightful. Our life becomes tedious, being spent in an impatient expectation of the joyous time when we will meet again. But if death has made the separation, as is inevitable, it results in a grief that all the misfortunes of human life can hardly equal. And in this circumstance, we may pay a high price for the comforts of our friendship. But oh! How happy are those who have placed their love on Him who can never be absent from them! They only need to open their eyes, and they will behold the traces of His presence and glory everywhere. They can always talk with the One their soul loves. This makes the darkest prison or wildest desert not only supportable, but delightful to them.

Loving God Makes Us Partake of an Infinite Happiness

In conclusion, a lover is miserable if the person he loves is miserable. Those who have made an exchange of hearts by love share in one another's happiness and misery. This makes love a troublesome passion when placed on earth. The most fortunate person has enough grief to mar the tranquility of his friend. It is hard to endure when we are attacked on all hands and suffer not only in our own lives, but also in another's.

But if God was the object of our love, we would share it in infinite happiness without any mixture or possibility of decrease. We would rejoice to behold the glory of God, and receive comfort and pleasure from all the praises of men and angels who extol him. It should delight us beyond all measure to consider that the beloved of our souls is infinitely happy in himself. And that all his enemies cannot shake or disturb his throne; "that our God is in the heavens, and does whatever he pleases."

Behold what a sure foundation his happiness is built on whose soul is possessed with love for God! The one who's will is transformed into the will of God! The one who's greatest desire is that his Maker should be pleased! Oh! The peace, the rest, and the satisfaction that accompanies this character of mind!

He Who Loves God Finds Sweetness in Every Circumstance

What an infinite pleasure it is to lose ourselves in Him, so that being swallowed up in the overwhelming sense of his goodness, we offer ourselves a living sacrifice continually ascending to him in flames of love. A soul never knows what solid joy and substantial pleasure is, until being weary of itself, it renounces all ownership and gives itself up to the Author of its being. It then feels that it has become a holy and devoted thing. Then it can say from an inward awareness and feeling, "My beloved is mine." I consider all his interest to be mine "and I am his." I am content to be anything for him. I don't care about myself, but only that I may serve him.

A person molded into this quality would find pleasure in all that God does and allows. Temporal enjoyments have another pleasure when he tastes the divine goodness in them, and considers them as tokens of love sent by his dearest Lord and Maker. Even though chastisements are not joyous but grievous, they would lose their sting in this frame of mind. The rod as well as the staff would comfort him. He would snatch a kiss from the hand that was smiting him, and gather sweetness from the severity. He would rejoice even though God did not do the will of such a worthless and foolish creature as himself. He would rejoice because God did his own will and accomplished his own designs, which are infinitely more holy and wise.

The Duties of Christianity Are Delightful to Him

The exercises of true Christianity, which to others are boring and tedious, yield the highest pleasure and delight to souls possessed with love for God. They rejoice when they are called "to go up to the house of the Lord that they may see his power and his glory, as they have previously seen it in the sanctuary." Their greatest joy comes when they have retired from the world, become free from the noise and hurry of life, silenced all their clamorous passions (those troublesome guests within), and have placed themselves in the presence of God. As they entertain fellowship and communion with him, they delight to adore his perfections, recount his favors, profess their affection to him, and tell him a thousand times that they love him. They delight in laying out their troubles or wants before him, and in finding release from the burdens of their hearts in his bosom. Repentance itself is a delightful exercise when it flows from the source of love. There is a secret sweetness which accompanies the tears of remorse, the tenderizing of the heart, the surrender of a soul returning to God, and the grieving over its former unkindness.

The strictness of a holy life, and the constant watch that we are obliged to keep over our hearts and ways are very troublesome to those who are only ruled and acted on by an external law, and have no law in their minds inclining them to the performance of their duty. But where love for God possesses the soul, it stands as a sentinel to keep out everything that may offend the beloved, and disdainfully repulses the temptations that assault it. It complies cheerfully, not only with explicit commands, but with the most secret notices of the beloved's pleasure. It is ingenious in discovering what will be most pleasing and acceptable to him. It makes mortification and self-denial change their harsh and dreadful names to become easy, sweet, and delightful things.

But I find this part of my book swelling bigger than I had planned. Indeed, who would not be tempted to dwell on so pleasant a theme? I shall endeavor to compensate by being brief in the other points.

The Excellence of Love for Others

The next branch of the Divine life is a universal charity and love. The excellence of this grace will be easily acknowledged. For what can be more noble and generous than a heart enlarged to embrace the whole world, whose wishes and plans are aimed at the good and welfare of the universe, and considers every man's interests to be his own? He who loves his neighbor as himself can never entertain any low or hurtful thought, or be lacking in acts of generosity. He would rather suffer a thousand wrongs than be guilty of one. He only considers himself happy when someone else has been benefitted by him. The malice or ingratitude of men is not able to defeat his love. He overlooks their injuries, pities their folly, and overcomes their evil with good. He never plots any other revenge against his most bitter and malicious enemies, other than putting all the debt of love he can upon them, even if they don't want it.

Is it any wonder that such a person is esteemed and admired and considered the darling of mankind? This inward goodness and gracious spirit imparts a sweetness and serenity upon the very countenance, and makes it friendly and lovely. It inspires the soul with a noble resoluteness and courage. It makes it capable of engaging and affecting the noblest things. Those heroic actions that we like to read about with admiration have, for the most part, been merely the effects of the love of one's own country or of a particular friendship. Certainly a more extensive and universal love must be much more powerful and active.

The Pleasure That Accompanies It

Again, as love flows from a noble and excellent character, so it is accompanied with the greatest satisfaction and pleasure. It delights the soul to feel the increased supply of love and to be delivered from the unsettling, as well as deformed passions. The soul rejoices as malice, hatred, and envy are also replaced with a gentle, sweet, and benign spirit. If I had my choice of anything that would bring me happiness, I would choose to have my heart possessed with the greatest kindness and affection towards all men in the world. I am sure this would make me partake in all the happiness of others. Their inward enrichments and outward prosperity, as well as everything that benefited and advantaged them, would bring me comfort and pleasure.

Even though I should frequently meet with occasions of grief and compassion, yet there is a sweetness in the sharing in the afflictions of others, which makes it infinitely more desirable than a brutish callousness. The consideration of the infinite goodness and wisdom that governs the world prevents excessive sorrow for tragedies that happen in it. The hope or possibility of men's eternal bliss moderates our sorrow for their present misfortunes. Certainly, second to the love and enjoyment of God, the ardent love and affection that blessed souls embrace others with is rightly considered the greatest joy of the heavenly places. If it universally prevailed in the world, it would be a precursor of that blessedness, and give us a taste of the joys of heaven on earth.

The Excellence of Purity

I called purity the third branch of real Christianity. You may remember that I defined it as contempt toward physical pleasures, and a resoluteness to face the troubles and pains we may meet with in the performance of our duty. Now, just its name is enough to recommend it as a most noble and excellent quality. There is no slavery as low as the slavery of a man who becomes a forced laborer to his own lusts. And there is no victory as glorious as the victory over them. It is impossible for the person who has sunk into the gross and feculent pleasures of sense, or has been bewitched with the worthless and illusionary gratifications of desire to do anything noble and worthy. But the soul inhabited by God is of a more sublime and divine character. It knows it was made for higher things, and vigorously rejects straying one step out of the ways of holiness in order to obtain any of these gratifications.

The Delight Purity Provides

And this purity is accompanied with a great deal of pleasure. Everything that defiles the soul disturbs it too. All impure delights have a sting in them, and leave hurt and trouble behind them. Excess, the absence of restraint, and all uncontrolled lusts are enemies to both the health of the body and to the interests of this present life. So much so, that a little consideration might oblige any rational man to shun them for this reason alone. If real Christians rise even higher than rational men, they not only abstain from noxious pleasures, but they neglect innocent pleasures too. This is not to be looked upon as an extreme or uncomfortable restraint, but as the result of a better choice. It indicates that their minds are occupied with the pursuit of higher and more refined delights. Therefore, they cannot be concerned with these things.

Any person that is engaged in an extreme and passionate desire will easily forget his ordinary gratifications. He will not give much attention to his diet, bodily comfort, or to the entertainments he was accustomed to delight in. It is no wonder that souls overpowered with a love for God despise inferior pleasures, and are almost ready to withhold from the body the necessities of life. They view all these things as impertinent to their highest happiness and to the higher enjoyments they are pursuing. They rejoice in the hardships they encounter as opportunities to exercise and demonstrate their love. Because they are able to do so little for God, the honor of suffering for him is a delight.

The Excellence of Humility

The last branch of real Christianity is humility. To

unregenerate and carnal eyes, humility appears an inferior, low, and despicable quality. But in reality, the soul of man is not capable of a higher and nobler endowment. It is foolish ignorance that gives birth to pride. But humility arises from a close acquaintance with excellent things. It keeps men from placing excessive attention on less important things or attainments. Noble and well-educated souls don't have a high opinion of riches, beauty, strength, and other advantages like these. Therefore, they don't base their evaluation of themselves on these things or despise those that lack them. They have an understanding of inner worth and real goodness. The awareness they have of the Divine perfections gives them a very low opinion of anything they have attained. So they continually strive to improve themselves and to become more like the infinite excellences they admire.

I don't know the thoughts people have concerning humility, but I see almost everyone pretending to have it. I see them shunning any expressions and actions that might cause them to be considered arrogant and presumptuous. Therefore, those who are most desirous of praise will be reluctant to commend themselves. Aren't all the expressions of respect and courtesy that are so common in our daily interactions, merely protests of the esteem of others and evidence of the low opinions we have of ourselves? Doesn't real humility have to be a noble and excellent endowment, when these shadows of it are considered a necessary part of a good upbringing?

The Pleasure and Sweetness of Humility

Again, the gift of humility is accompanied with an abundance of happiness and tranquility. The proud and arrogant person is a pain to all who interact with him, but even more to himself. Everything upsets him and hardly anything is capable of satisfying and pleasing him. He is ready to complain about everything that doesn't go his way. It is as if he were so important that God Almighty should do everything to gratify him, and all the creatures of heaven and earth should wait upon him and obey his will.

The leaves of high trees shake with every blast of wind; and every breath and every evil word will upset and torment an arrogant man. But the humble person has the advantage when he is despised. None can have a lower opinion than he does of himself. Therefore, he is not troubled by these things and can easily bear reproaches that would wound the other to the soul. Indeed, because he is less affected with injuries, he is less likely to be harmed by them. "Contention, which comes from pride," betrays a man into a thousand troubles that those of a meek and lowly quality rarely encounter. True and genuine humility brings both admiration and love from all wise and discerning persons. But pride defeats its own intentions and deprives a man of the honor it deceives him into claiming.

Because the "primary exercises of humility" are those that relate to Almighty God, they are accompanied by the greatest satisfaction and sweetness. It is impossible to express the great pleasure and delight that real Christians feel in the lowest prostration of their souls before God. Having a deep sense of the Divine majesty and glory, they sink to the bottom of their being, vanishing and ceasing to exist in the presence of God. This is facilitated by a serious and affectionate acknowledgment of their own nothingness, and the insufficiencies and imperfections of their attainments. They understand the full sense and emphasis of the Psalmist's exclamation, "Lord, what is man" and can say it with the same affection. The humble, godly man denounces the praises and applauses of men with far more pleasure than the haughty and ambitious man has in receiving it. "Not to us, O Lord, not to us, but to your name give glory," etc.

So I have written of the excellence and advantage of real Christianity in its several branches. But if I pretend to have given a complete description, I will be doing great harm to the subject. Let us become familiar with it, my dear friend, let us become familiar with it. Then experience will teach us more than all that has ever been spoken or written concerning it. But if we believe that our soul has already been awakened to longing desires for this great blessedness, it will be good to release them, and allow them to flow in aspirations like these.

A Prayer

"Good God! What a great joy we are called to! How graciously you have joined our duty and happiness together, and designed that the performance of our work is a great reward! And shall such silly worms be advanced to such a great height? Will you allow us to raise our eyes to you? Will you admit and accept our affection? Shall we receive the impression of your divine excellences by beholding and admiring them, and partake of your infinite blessedness and glory by loving you and rejoicing in them? Oh! There is great happiness in the souls that have broken the chains of self-love, and have untangled their affection from every confining and incomplete good! Those whose minds are enlightened by the Holy Spirit and their wills increased to the extent of your will! Those who love you above all things and all mankind for your sake!

"I am persuaded, O God, I am persuaded that I can never be happy until my carnal and corrupt affections are mortified, and the pride and vanity of my spirit are subdued. Until I begin to seriously despise the world and no longer think about myself. But, oh! When will it happen! Oh! When will you come to me and satisfy my soul with your likeness, making me holy as you are holy, even in every aspect of life! Have you given me a prospect of so great a joy and will you not bring me into it? Have you excited these desires in my soul and will you not satisfy them too? Oh! Teach me to do your will, for you are my God. Your Spirit is good. Lead me into the land of righteousness. Breathe life into me, O Lord, for your name's sake. Complete what pertains to me. Your mercy, O Lord, endures forever; do not forsake the works of your hands."

Part Three

The Hopeless Thoughts of Some Newly Awakened to a Proper Perspective

I have described the nature of true Christianity and how desirable it is. But when someone sees how infinitely distant it is from the common character and mindset of men, he may be ready to give up hope and give in to the thought that it is utterly impossible to attain. He may sit down in sadness, bemoan himself, and say in the anguish and bitterness of his spirit, "They are happy indeed whose souls are awakened to the divine life and are renewed in the spirit of their minds. But alas! I am very different and am not able to produce this big change. If outward observances could have produced it, I might have hoped to prove myself worthy by diligence and care. But because only a new nature can make this change, what am I able to do? I could give all my goods in offerings to God or alms to the poor. But because I cannot master true love and charity this expense would profit me nothing. This gift of God cannot be purchased with money. If a man should give all the substance of his house for love, it would be utterly despised. I could punish my body, waste away through excessive fasting, and undergo many hardships and troubles. But I cannot starve all my corruptions to death or totally wean all my affections from earthly things. There are still some worldly desires lurking in my heart, and when I shut the door on any of these empty things they get back into my life through the windows.

"I am frequently convinced of my own inferiority, the weakness of my body, and the far greater weakness of my soul. But this causes indignation and discontent instead of true humility in my spirit. Even though I may consider myself inferior, yet I cannot accept that others would see me as inferior also. When I reflect on my highest and most visible attainments, I have reason to suspect that they are only the deeds of the carnal nature; that is, the manifestations of self-love acting under several disguises. This nature is so powerful and so deeply rooted in me, that I can never hope to be delivered from the dominion of it. I may toss and turn as a door on its hinges, but I can never get free or truly unhinged of self. It is still the center of all my actions. Therefore, all the advantage I can draw from the discovery of real Christianity is only to see the great unreachable joy and happiness from a long distance. I'm like a shipwrecked man who sees the land and envies the happiness of those who are there, while thinking it is impossible to get ashore."

The Unreasonableness of These Fears

Desponding thoughts like these may arise in the minds of people who begin to understand more of the nature and excellence of real Christianity. They have spied the land and have seen that it is exceedingly good, that it flows with milk and honey. But they find they have the children of Anak to grapple with, many powerful lusts and corruptions to overcome, and they fear they will never prevail against them. But why should we give way to such discouraging suggestions? Why should we entertain such unreasonable fears that dampen our spirits, weaken our hands, and increase the difficulties of our way?

Let us encourage ourselves my dear friend, let us encourage ourselves with the mighty provisions we are to expect in this spiritual warfare, for greater is he that is for us than all that can rise up against us. "The eternal God is our refuge" and underneath this refuge are the everlasting arms. Let us be strong in the Lord and the power of his might, for he shall tread down our enemies. God has a tender regard for the souls of men and is infinitely willing to promote their welfare. He has willingly stooped to our weakness and declared with an oath that he takes no pleasure in our destruction. There isn't anything like malice or envy lodged in the heart of the ever-blessed Being whose name and nature is Love.

He created us in a happy condition and now that we have fallen from it, "He has granted help to one that is mighty to save." He has committed the care of our souls to no less than the eternal Son of his love. It is he that is the captain of our salvation. What enemies can be too strong for us when we are fighting under his banner? Didn't the Son of God come down from the bosom of his Father and pitch his tent among the sons of men in order to restore and propagate the divine life, and restore the image of God in their souls? All the mighty works that Jesus performed and all the sorrowful afflictions he sustained had this for their object and design. It was for this he labored and toiled. For this he bled and died. "He was with child, he was in pain, and has he brought forth nothing but wind, has he not worked deliverance on the earth? Shall he not see the results of the travail of his soul?"

Certainly it is impossible for this great design of heaven to prove abortive, that such a mighty undertaking should fail and miscarry. It has already been effectual for the salvation of many thousands who were just as far from the kingdom of heaven as we may think we are. Our "High priest continues forever, and is able to save to the extreme those who come to God through him." He is tender and compassionate, knows our infirmities, and has experienced our temptations. "He will not break a bruised reed and not quench a smoldering wick, until he sends forth judgment into victory."

He has sent out his Holy Spirit, who's sweet but powerful breathings are still moving throughout the world, to bring life and revive the souls of men. The Holy Spirit awakens souls to the understanding and feeling of the divine things they were created to enjoy. He is ready to assist weak and despairing creatures, like us, in our efforts towards holiness and fullness of joy in Christ. When he has begun to take hold of a soul and has kindled in it the smallest spark of divine love, he will be sure to preserve, cherish, and set it ablaze. This is a fire "that many waters shall not quench and the floods will not be able to drown." When this day begins to dawn "and the daystar arises in the heart," he will easily dispel the powers of darkness and make ignorance, folly, and all the corrupt and selfish affections of men flee away as fast as the shades of night when the sun comes out of his chamber. For "the path of the just is as the shining light, which shines brighter and brighter until the full day." "They shall go on from strength to increasing strength until every one of them appears before God in Zion."

Why should we think it's impossible for true goodness and universal love to come, to both govern and prevail in our souls? Isn't this their original state and condition, their native and genuine quality as they came from the hands of their Maker? Sin and corruption are only usurpers, and although they have held possession for a long time, "from the beginning it was not so."

The unregulated self-love, that one would think was rooted in our very being and interwoven with the quality of our nature, is nevertheless of foreign lineage, and had no place at all in the healthy state of being. We are still intelligent enough to condemn it. Our understandings are easily convinced that we should be wholly devoted to Him from whom we have our being. And to love the One who is infinitely better than us, infinitely more than ourselves. Our wills would readily comply with this if they were not disordered and put out of tune. Isn't he who made our souls able to rectify and mend them again? Won't we be able by his assistance to vanquish and expel those violent intruders, "and cause the armies of the aliens to flee?"

No sooner shall we take up arms in this holy war, but we shall have all the saints on earth, and all the angels in heaven engaged on our behalf. The holy Church throughout the world is interceding daily with God for the success of all these endeavors. Without a doubt, the heavenly hosts above are equally concerned with the interests of real Christianity, and infinitely desirous to see the Divine life thriving and prevailing in this inferior world. They want the will of God to be done by us on earth as it is done by them in heaven. Therefore, shouldn't we encourage ourselves, as the prophet did his servant, when he showed him the horses and chariots of fire? "Fear not, for those who are with us are more than those who are against us."

We Must Do What We Can Depending on the Assistance of God

Therefore, put away all perplexing fears and desponding thoughts. The largest part of the conquest is our undertaking it vigorously, and relying confidently on divine assistance. "Let us arise and take action, and the Lord will be with us." Yes it is true; real Christianity in the souls of men is solely the work of God. And it is true that all our natural endeavors can't produce it alone, or earn the supernatural aids that produce it. The Holy Ghost must come upon us and the power of the Most High must overshadow us before the holy life is birthed and Christ is formed in us. But we must not expect that the complete work will be accomplished without any cooperating effort of our own. We must not lie loitering in the ditch waiting until Omnipotence pulls us out. No, no! We must arouse ourselves and actuate the powers that we have already received. We must exert ourselves to our utmost capacities. Then we may hope that "our labor shall not be in vain in the Lord."

All the science and industry of man cannot form the smallest herb or make a stalk of corn grow in the field without starting with a seed or a living part. It is the energy of life and the influences of heaven that produce life. It is God "who causes the grass to grow for livestock and plants to grow for man's cultivation." Even so, nobody will say that the labors of the farmer are useless or unnecessary. In the same way, the human soul is solely created by God. It is he who both forms and gives life to the child. Yet, God has appointed the marriage-bed as the ordinary means for the propagation of mankind.

Even though the touch of Omnipotence must intervene to cause the mighty change of new life in our souls, we should do what we can to become proper vessels and to prepare ourselves. We must break up our fallow ground, root out the weeds, and pull up the thorns so that we may be better prepared to receive the seeds of grace and the dew of heaven.

It is true that God has been found by some who didn't seek him. He has thrown himself in the path of some who were far from his path. He has grabbed hold of them and instantly stopped them in their tracks. That's what he did when Paul was converted on his journey to Damascus. But certainly this is not God's ordinary method of dealing with men. Though he hasn't tied himself to human efforts, he has tied us to the use of them. We will never have a better reason to expect divine assistance than when we are giving our best efforts.

Therefore, my next effort will be to show the course we should take in order to acquire the blessed character I have described so far. If in delivering my own thoughts on this subject I happen to differ from what is said by others in this matter, I don't want you to think that I contradict and oppose them. It may be the same as when physicians prescribe differing remedies for the same disease. They may all be useful and good, and therefore are not conflicting. Everyone may propose the method he believes to be the most proper and convenient, but he does not pretend that the cure can only be affected if his method is precisely followed.

I am convinced that some holy people have been unnecessarily perplexed to a great degree because they have not seen the typical orderly progression in their souls as described in some books. They have not passed through all the steps and stages of conversion recorded by some who "may have prescribed what they had personally experienced as the only way." God has several ways of dealing with the souls of men and all that matters is that the work is accomplished, regardless of the methods used.

In proposing instructions, I must follow the order that the inherent character of the subject implies. But I do not mean that this method should be observed sequentially in its application. The latter rules are not to be ignored until considerable time has been spent in practicing the former. These Instructions are mutually conducive to one another, and all of them are to be performed as appropriate and as God's grace is supplied.

We Must Avoid Every Kind of Sin

But now I will not delay the practical instructions any longer. If we desire to have our souls molded into this holy life, to become partakers of the Divine nature, and have Christ formed in our hearts, we must seriously resolve and carefully endeavor to avoid and abandon all malicious and sinful practices. There can't be a treaty of peace with God until we lay down these weapons of rebellion that attack heaven. Nor can we expect to have our corrupted nature cured if we are feeding daily on poison. Every willful sin gives a mortal wound to the soul and puts it at a greater distance from God and goodness. We can never hope to have our hearts purified from corrupt desires, unless we cleanse our hands from malicious actions.

Now, in this case, we cannot excuse ourselves by claiming that it's impossible. This is so because there is no doubt that our outward man is under some degree of our control. We have some command of our feet, hands, and tongue. Yes, and of our thoughts and desires too, at least to the extent that we can divert them from impure and sinful objects, and put our attention somewhere else. We will find this power and authority strengthened considerably and expanded if we are careful to manage and exercise it. At the same time, I acknowledge that because our corruptions are so strong and our temptations so many, that it will require a great deal of steadfastness, resoluteness, watchfulness, and care to maintain ourselves in this degree of innocence and purity.

We Must Know What Things Are Sinful

In order to pursue holiness, we must begin by thoroughly educating ourselves regarding what sins we must abstain from. And here we must not take our standards from the principles of the world or the practices of those we, in being generous, call good men. Most people have a very shallow comprehension of these things and are not aware of any sinfulness, unless it is shameful and scandalous. They barely consider any sin as great as what they call nitpicking. Those who are more serious usually allow themselves too much latitude and freedom.

Alas! How much pride, vanity, passion, impulsiveness, weakness, folly, and sin are manifested daily in their words and behavior? It may be they are humbled because of it, are striving against it, and are daily gaining some ground. But because they make very little progress and their failings are so many, we have to choose a better pattern.

We must all answer for ourselves. The practices of others will never excuse and justify us. It is the highest folly to regulate our actions by any other standard than the one we will be judged by. If we could ever "cleanse our way," it must be "by taking heed to the word of God." We must look to the "word that is alive and powerful, sharper than any two-edged sword." It is "even able to distinguish the difference between soul and spirit, of the joints and marrow and exposes the thoughts and intentions of the heart." Then we will certainly discover that many things that pass as totally innocent in the eyes of the world, are actually sinful and heinous.

Let us therefore imitate the Psalmist, who said, "Concerning the works of men, by the words of your lips I have kept myself from the paths of the destroyer." Let us acquaint ourselves with the strict and holy laws of our faith. Let us consider the teachings of our blessed Savior, especially the divine Sermon on the Mount. Take in the writings of his holy apostles, where an intelligent and unbiased mind can clearly discern the limits and boundaries that should govern our actions. Then let us never look upon any sin as light and trivial. We are to be fully persuaded that the smallest sin is infinitely heinous in the sight of God and harmful to the souls of men. If we have corrected eyesight, we will be as deeply affected with our smallest irregularities as we are with the worst crimes.

We Must Resist the Temptations to Sin by Considering the Evils They Will Bring on Us

Because of our individual personalities, habits, and desires in this world, we will find that some of the things that we discover to be sinful have been deeply wedded to our lives. We have become one with these to the extent that our turning from them will seem like cutting off our right hands or plucking out our right eyes. Because of this seemingly impossible task, do we now throw up our hands and wait for these attachments to go away by themselves? Taking this course of action is imitating the poet's fool who stood all day on the riverbank waiting for all the water to pass. We must not pamper our inclinations as we would a little child, waiting for them to grow tired of the thing they are unwilling to let go. We must not continue our sinful practices in hopes that the grace of God will eventually overpower our spirits and cause us to hate these practices because they are hideous.

Let us suppose the worst, that we are completely lacking supernatural assistance and the spiritual taste buds that discern and abhor perverse things. Yet we are surely capable of sound reasoning that may have the power to persuade us to reform our lives. If this inward deformity and heinous nature of sin isn't enough to change us, at least we may be frightened by the dreadful consequences that come with sin. Then the same selfish nature that pushes us forward in the pursuit of sinful pleasures will make us detest the thought of paying the price of everlasting misery. In this way, we may attack self-love with its own weapons and employ one natural inclination to repress the excesses of another.

Let us, therefore, make a habit of serious consideration of what a fearful thing it must be to irritate and offend the infinite Being. He is the only one who can keep us from everlasting destruction and the one we depend on every moment. He can make us miserable by simply withdrawing his mercies or make us nothing by withdrawing his assistance.

Let us regularly consider how short and uncertain our lives are, and how that after we have taken a few trips around the sun on this world, and lived a little longer among men, we must all go down into the dark and silent grave. We will carry nothing along with us except anguish and regret for all our sinful enjoyments. Then consider what horror must seize the guilty soul as it finds itself naked and all alone before the severe and impartial Judge of the world. He will render an exact account, not only of one's more important and considerable transactions, but of every word from the tongue and the most secret and fleeting thought that ever passed through the mind.

Let us picture the terrors of that dreadful day when the foundation of the earth will be shaken, the heavens will pass away with a great noise, the elements will melt with fervent heat, and the present fabric of nature will dissolve. Then our eyes will see the blessed Jesus who previously came into the world in all humility to visit us, purchase pardon for us, and strongly encourage us to accept it. Picture him now, appearing in the majesty of his glory and descending from heaven in a flaming fire to take vengeance on those that have despised his mercy, and have persisted in their rebellion against his will. Picture what it will be like when all the things done in secret are brought to light, and the imaginations and plans of the heart are exposed. All of the secret impurities and subtle deceptions that no one ever suspected of us will be exposed and presented for public viewing. Thousands of actions that we never dreamed were sinful, or that we had forgotten will be charged against us to remain in our consciences. These charges will come with such evident convictions of guilt that we will not be able to deny or excuse them.

On judgement day all the angels in heaven and all the saints that ever lived on the earth will approve the dreadful sentence that will be passed on wicked men. Now that the truth has been exposed, those who may have loved and esteemed them in the world will now look upon them with indignation and abhorrence, without making any requests for their deliverance.

Let us consider the eternal punishment of damned souls that are foreshadowed in scripture by metaphors illustrated with the things that are extremely terrible and distressful in the world. And even these are not adequate to give us the full weight and terror of this eternal state. After we have combined all of these expressions and have pictured them in our minds, as best as we can conceive of misery and torment we must still remember that all this comes infinitely short of its truth and reality.

It is true that this is a sad and depressing subject. There is anguish and horror in the consideration of it. But without any doubt it must be infinitely more dreadful to endure it. Considering these things may be very useful to scare us away from the paths that would lead us there. Regardless of how fond we may be of sinful pleasures, the fear of hell would make us abstain. Our strongest habits will be shocked and undone when in the olive press of the prophet's question, "Who among us can dwell with everlasting burnings?"

It is for this reason that the terrors of another world are so frequently represented in the Bible with terms that are most appropriate to affect and influence a carnal mind. These fears are not sufficient to make anyone truly good. But they can certainly restrain us from a lot of evil, and have often laid a foundation for more intelligent and beneficial changes.

We Must Keep a Constant Watch Over Ourselves

Considering these things from time to time is not enough. Neither is making resolutions about forsaking our sins. We must also maintain a constant guard and be continually watching against them. Sometimes the mind is awakened to see the dismal consequences of a depraved life and immediately we resolve to reform. But alas! It quickly falls asleep and we lose the opportunity we had. Then temptations take the advantage by continually soliciting and persistently begging. Therefore, they frequently get us to comply before we know it.

It is the folly and ruin of most people to live for adventure, taking part in everything that comes their way. They seldom consider what they are about to say or do. If we want our resolutions to have any effect, we must take heed to our ways and set a guard before the door of our lips. We must cross examine the impulses that arise in our hearts, and get them to tell us where they come from and where they will lead us. Then we can discern whether it is pride, passion, or any corrupt and malicious attitude that motivates us. Then we can know whether God will be offended, or if someone may be harmed by it.

And if we don't have time to stop and think it through, let us at least turn our eyes toward God. We can place ourselves in his presence asking his permission and approval for what we do. Let us recognize that we are under the all-seeing eye of the Divine Majesty as if illuminated by a spot light. To him all things are visible including the past, the future, and the innermost recesses of our souls. The awareness of, and continual focus on the Divine Presence, are the most available and effective tools to both discover what is unlawful and to restrain us from it. There are some things that a person could alter in order to cover them up with excuses or to rationalize them away, and yet he won't dare to look Almighty God in the face and adventure upon them.

If we look to Him we will be enlightened. "If we set him always before us, he will guide us by his eye, and instruct us in the way in which we ought to walk."

We Must Examine Our Actions Regularly

This care and watchfulness over our actions must be accompanied by the frequent and serious reflection of them. This is necessary if we want to obtain Divine mercy and pardon for our sins through the humble and sorrowful acknowledgment of them. It is also important if we want to reinforce and strengthen our resolutions, and learn to resist and say no to the temptations that have foiled us in the past.

The following advice, even though it was written by an unbeliever, is worthy of a Christian. Before we fall asleep at night, we should remember and examine all the events of the day. In this way we may be encouraged by what we have done right, and may correct what we recognize as having missed the mark. We can make the shipwrecks of today into the danger signs to direct our course tomorrow. This may be called the very art of virtuous living. It will make a significant contribution to the advancement of our reformation and the preservation of our innocence.

But in the practice of these things, we must not forget to ask God to assist us. This is especially important against the sins that we struggle with the most. Even though our hearts may tell us that we haven't become the new creations that would make our devotions acceptable to God, these suggestions to help us turn from sin may influence our natural man to become serious about seeking the new birth. This would make our prayers against sin as serious and intense as our prayers against other calamities.

I am convinced that God, who hears the cry of the ravens, will have some regard even for petitions that proceed from the natural desires that he has implanted in us. These prayers against sin will also produce commitment in us, encouraging us to watchfulness and care. Common honesty will make us too ashamed to relapse into the faults we have recently bewailed before God, and have begged him to help us get the victory over.

Restraint in Lawful Things is Healthy

So it is by the restraint of our natural inclinations that we begin our efforts to recover the divine life. Restraint keeps these inclinations from breaking out in sinful practices. But now I must add that Christian wisdom will teach us to abstain from gratifications that are not unlawful in themselves. We do this for more than securing our innocence that would be constantly threatened when we push the limits of our liberty. Through our restraint, we weaken the power of our natural man and teach our appetites to obey. Wise parents will deny the will of their children in many little things in order to develop them into children who are more manageable and submissive in more important situations. We must apply this same wisdom to ourselves by restraining the will of our natural man.

He who desires to mortify the pride and vanity of his spirit should stop his ears to the most deserved praises. He should often restrain himself from seeking his just vindication from the criticisms and slanders of others. This is especially important if they merely reflect on his wisdom and conduct, and not on his purity and innocence. He who desires to check a revengeful temperament would gain ground by denying himself the satisfaction of relating his injuries to others. If we want to take heed to our ways to the extent that we don't sin with our tongue, we must extensively acclimate ourselves to solitude and silence. We must at times, with the Psalmist, "Hold our peace even from good," until we finally acquire some control over that unruly member. Therefore, we may take our natural inclinations captive and make our appetites more moderate in their cravings by acclimating them to frequent refusals. Yet it is not enough to have them under abuse and restraint.

We Must Strive to Put Ourselves Out of Love With the World

Our next course of action must be to wean our affections from created things, and all the delights and entertainments of this lower life. These things sink and depress the souls of men and retard their efforts toward God and heaven. To accomplish this, we must take charge of our minds with a deep persuasion of the vanity and emptiness of worldly enjoyments. This is an ordinary theme, and everybody can elaborate on this subject. But alas! How few understand and believe what they say? These notions float in our brains and come sliding off our tongues, but we don't have a deep impression of them on our spirits. We don't have any conviction of the truth that we pretend to believe.

We can recognize that all the glory, splendor, pleasures, and enjoyments of the world are vanity and nothing. Yet these nothings take up all our thoughts and engross all our affections. They stifle the better inclinations of the soul and lead us into many a sin. It may be that we take this issue seriously sometimes, and choose to ignore them and resolve not to be deluded with them anymore. But these corrections of our course seldom outlive the next temptation. The vanities that we have shut the front door on, sneak in through the back gate.

We still harbor some claims to our rights and freedoms to these things, and some hopes that flatter us into seeking after them again. Even after we have been frustrated a thousand times, we continue to repeat this frustrating and empty way of life. The smallest difference in the circumstances is enough to delude us and make us expect that satisfaction will come this time, even though it didn't last time. If we could break free from this delusion and come to a real and serious contempt of worldly things, we would make real progress in our relationship with God.

The soul of man has a lively and active nature and possesses a raging and inextinguishable thirst, an immaterial kind of fire. It is always reaching for one object or another, thinking that it will bring happiness. If the soul was torn from the world and all the bewitching enjoyments under the sun, it would quickly search after some higher and more excellent object to satisfy its passionate and persistent cravings. And no longer being dazzled with glittering vanities, it would cling to that supreme and All-sufficient Good, where it would discover incredible beauty and sweetness that would charm and overpower all its affections.

The love of the world and the love of God are like the scales of a balance. As the one falls, the other rises. When our natural inclinations run our lives and self is exalted in our soul, our spiritual life lacks conviction and becomes weak. But when earthly objects wither away and lose their beauty, and the soul begins to lose its passion and interest in pursuing them, the seeds of grace take root and the Divine life begins to flourish and prevail.

Therefore, this realization should lead us to apply diligence in convincing ourselves of the emptiness and vanity of creature-enjoyments. Therefore, we must reason our hearts out of love with them. Let us seriously consider all that our reason, faith, and experience, as well as all the observations of others, can suggest to this effect. Let us ponder the matter over and over, fixing our thoughts on this truth until we are thoroughly persuaded to live it.

Amidst all our pursuits and plans, let us stop and ask ourselves the right questions. What is the goal of all this? What am I aiming at? Can the gross polluted pleasures of sense, a heap of white and yellow earth (silver and gold), or the esteem and affection of silly creatures like me satisfy a rational and immortal soul? Haven't I tried these things already? Will they bring more enjoyment and yield more contentment tomorrow than they have in the past? What will be different next year that could possibly make any difference in the end results of pursuing the things of this world?

There may be a little difference between what I am now pursuing and what I enjoyed before. But I must remember that it is always the same in one respect. Before I attained the former enjoyments, they also appealed to me with the appearance of pleasure to come and promised to be worthy of my pursuit. But, like the rainbow, they looked very glorious at a distance, but when I approached I found nothing but emptiness and vapor. Oh! What a poor existence we would have if we weren't capable of any higher enjoyments!

I cannot persist on this subject, and when I remember to whom I am writing, there is little need to continue. Yes, my dear friend, you have had a great degree of experience with the emptiness and vanity of human things. You now have very few worldly attachments, and I don't know of anyone with less. I have reflected on those passages of your life that you have confided to me. And through it all, I can see the design of the Divine Providence to wean your affections from everything here below. The trials you have had with the things that the world dotes upon have taught you to despise them. And you have learned through experience that neither one's natural abilities, nor the advantages of wealth are sufficient for happiness.

You have found that every rose has its thorn, and that there may be a worm at the root of the fairest gourd. Although some admire or envy the supposed happiness of the rich and famous, there is some secret and unseen grief that deserves pity instead. If any earthly comforts have had too much of your heart, I think they have been your family and friends. But the dearest of these have been taken out of the world, so that you must raise your mind toward heaven when you think of them. Therefore, God has provided a way for your heart to be liberated from the world, and that he will not have any rival in your affection. I have always observed that your affection is so large, universal, noble, and unselfish that no inferior object can respond equally, or be deserving of it.

We Must Do Those Outward Actions That Are Commanded

After we have begun to restrain our corruptions,

natural appetites, and inclinations toward worldly things, we must begin to do the things that have a more immediate tendency to excite and awaken the Divine life. To begin this process, let us endeavor to conscientiously perform the duties that real Christianity requires and would produce in us, if it prevailed in our souls. If we cannot acquire the change to our inward character now, let us at least study to regulate our outward behavior.

If our hearts haven't been set on fire with love for God yet, let us validate our allegiance to that Infinite Majesty anyway. We can do this by attending his service, listening to his Word, speaking reverently of his name, praising his goodness, and exhorting others to serve and obey him. If we lack that love and the heart of compassion that we should have toward our neighbors, we must still take advantage of any opportunity to do good. Even if our hearts are haughty and proud, we must study modest and humble behavior.

These external performances are of little value in themselves, yet they may help us move forward to better things. The Apostle indeed tells us, "bodily discipline profits little," but he doesn't say it is altogether useless. It is always good to be doing what we can, for then God is likely to pity our weakness and assist our feeble endeavors. And when true love, humility, and the other graces of the Divine Spirit come to take root in our souls, they will flow more freely. There will be less difficulty later, if we are already in the habit of expressing them in our outward interactions with others. We shouldn't fear the accusation of hypocrisy, even though our actions are, in this way, ahead of our affections. They are still proceeding from an awareness of our duty and our intention is not to appear better than we are, but to really become better.

We Must Endeavour to Form Internal Acts of Devotion, Charity, Etc.

Because inward acts have a more immediate influence on the soul, to mold it to a right quality and character, we must be consistent and diligent in the performance of them. Let us be regularly lifting up our hearts toward God. If we do not say that we love him above all things, let us at least acknowledge that it is our duty and would be our joy. Let us lament the dishonor done to him by foolish and sinful men, and applaud the praises and adorations that are given to him by the blessed and glorious multitude above. Let us surrender and yield ourselves up to him a thousand times, to be governed by his laws and to have our lives arranged according to his pleasure.

Even though our stubborn hearts should shrink back and rebel, let us tell him we are convinced that his will is always just and good. Therefore, we can tell him that our desire is for him to do whatever he pleases with us regardless of our will. Therefore, in order to create a universal charity toward men in us, we must be regularly desiring happiness for them and blessing every person that we see. And when we have done something for the relief of the distressed, we may second it with sincere desires that God would take care of them and deliver them out of all their troubles.

In this way we should exercise ourselves for godliness. When we are employing the powers that we have, the Spirit of God is ready to assist us and elevate these acts of our soul beyond the level of the natural man, giving them a divine impression. As a result of our frequent and persistent repetitions, we shall find ourselves more inclined to do them so that they flow with greater freedom and ease.

Contemplation is a Great Exercise of Real Christianity

I will mention only two more exercises for acquiring the holy and divine character of spirit that we have been considering. The first is a deep and serious contemplation of the truths of real Christianity. Both the certainty and importance of these truths are to be considered in this way. The attention typically given to divine truth is barely perceptible, lacking effort, very weak, and accomplishes very little. It only flows from a blind inclination to follow the religious ideas and practices that are in fashion, or a lazy indifference and lack of concern for whether these things are true or not.

Men are unwilling to disagree with the religious opinions of their upbringing. Because they believe all their fellow churchgoers are real Christians, they are content to remain in that condition. They rarely put forth serious effort to consider the evidences of the truths they hold, or to ponder their significance and claims. Therefore, their religion has very little influence on their affections and practice. Those "spiritless and paralytic thoughts," as one correctly called them, are not able to move the will and direct the hand.

Therefore, we must consciously and diligently apply ourselves to develop a serious belief in and a full persuasion of divine truths. We must do this until we develop a perception of and sensitivity to spiritual things. Our thoughts must dwell upon them until we are both convinced of them and deeply affected by them. Let us urge our spirits forward and force them to approach the invisible world. Let us fix our minds on immaterial things until we clearly perceive that they are not dreams. No, they are not. Truth is, everything else is nothing but dreams and shadows.

When we look around and behold the beauty and magnificence of this spectacular universe, and the order and harmony of the whole creation, let our thoughts fly to the Omnipotent Wisdom and Goodness, who produced it in the beginning and continues to establish and uphold it. When we reflect on who we are, let us consider that we are not merely a piece of organized matter or just some amazing and marvelous organism. We must recognize that there is more to us than flesh, blood, and bones – the divine spark, capable of knowing, loving, and enjoying our Maker.

In this world, our souls and spirits are severely hindered by their ignorant and cumbersome physical companion (our flesh). Even so, they will be delivered soon. Then they can exist without the body, like we can without the clothes that we throw off whenever we want. Therefore, let us regularly withdraw our thoughts from this earth, this scene of misery, folly, and sin. Raise them toward the world that is more vast and glorious. See the world where innocent and blessed inhabitants eternally bask in comfort and joy in the Divine Presence, whose only emotions are an unadulterated joy and an unlimited love. And then consider how the blessed Son of God came down to this lower world to live among us, and die for us so that he might bring us to partake of the same blessedness. Ponder how he has overcome the sting of death, opened the kingdom of heaven to all true believers, and is sitting at the "right hand of the Majesty on high." Wonder that even though he is there, he is still just as aware of us and is receiving our prayers, presenting them to his Father. He is still visiting his Church daily with the influences of his Spirit, like the sun reaches us with its rays.

To Acquire Love for God We Must Consider the Excellence of His Nature

The serious and frequent consideration of these and other similar divine truths, is the most proper method to acquire the living faith that is the foundation of real Christianity, and the fountain and root of the Divine life. Let me also suggest some other subjects of meditation for producing its many branches.

And first, to set our souls on fire with the love for God, let us consider the excellence of his nature and his lovingkindness toward us. We don't know much of the Divine perfections. Even so, the little bit we do know may be sufficient to fill our souls with admiration and love to captivate our affections and to increase our awe of him.

We are not merely creatures of the physical senses that we should be incapable of any other affections except those that enter by the eyes. The character of any excellent person, whom we have never seen, will often engage our hearts and cause us to become thoroughly concerned with all his interests. And I ask what causes us to become so connected with those we do interact with? I cannot believe that it is merely the color of their face or their attractive appearance. If that is all there was to it, we would fall in love with statues, pictures, and flowers.

These outward characteristics may delight the eye to a small extent. But they would never be able to have so much of an impact on the heart if they did not represent some vital perfection. We either see or recognize some greatness of mind, strength of spirit, or sweetness of heart. Or there is a liveliness, wisdom, or goodness that charms our spirit and captivates our love. Now these perfections are not obvious to the sight. The eyes can only discern the indicators of their existence and their resultant actions.

If understanding directs the affections, and essential perfections are the predominant influence on them, then certainly the excellence of the Divine nature and its traces we discover in everything we behold would not fail to engage our hearts, if we seriously view and consider them. Wouldn't we be infinitely more enraptured with the almighty wisdom and goodness that fills the universe, displays itself in every part of the creation, establishes the frame of nature, turns the mighty gears of his sovereign will, and keeps the world from disorder and ruin? Do the faint rays of the very same perfections that we meet with in our fellow creatures even come close? Will we dote on the scattered pieces of a rude and imperfect picture, and never be affected with the original beauty? This would be an unaccountable stupidity and blindness. Whatever we find lovely in a friend or in a saint shouldn't capture our attention, but should elevate our affection beyond them. We should conclude that if there is so much sweetness in a drop, there must be infinitely more in the fountain. If there is such splendor in a ray, what must the sun be in its glory!

We cannot falsely claim the remoteness of the object as an excuse either, as if God is too far away for our fellowship or our love. "He is not far from every one of us, for in him we live, move, and have our being." We cannot open our eyes without seeing some traces of his glory. We cannot turn them toward him and not find that he is certainly watching us, waiting for us to look at him, and ready to entertain the most intimate fellowship and communion with us. Therefore, let us endeavor to lift our minds to the clearest comprehension of the Divine nature. Let us consider all that His works declare and all that his Word reveals about him.

And let us especially contemplate the visible representation of his character that was made in our own form. That is, his Son, who was "the radiance of his glory, and the exact image of his character." He is the One who appeared in the world to clearly reveal what God is like, and to be the example of how we should live. Let us bring him clearly before our minds, exactly as we find him described in the Gospels. It is there that we will behold the perfections of the Divine nature, although covered with the veil of human weakness. Let us frame the clearest notion that we are capable of regarding a being who is infinite in power, wisdom, and goodness, and who is the author and fountain of all perfection. Then let us fix the eyes of our soul upon him, so that our eyes may affect our heart, and the fire will burn as we contemplate his true nature.

We Should Meditate on His Goodness and Love

If we add the consideration of God's favor and goodwill toward us, the fire within will blaze especially bright. There is nothing more powerful for engaging our affection than finding that we are beloved. Expressions of kindness are always pleasing and acceptable to us, even if the person is usually mean and contemptible. But how it must astonish and delight us to have the love of one who is altogether lovely, and to know that the glorious Majesty of heaven has any regard for us! Oh, how it must overcome our spirits, melt our hearts, and put our whole soul on fire!

Just as the Word of God is full of the expressions of his love toward man, so all his works now proclaim it loudly. He gave us our existence, and through preserving us he repeats this giving every moment. He has placed us in a rich and well-furnished world, and has liberally provided for all our necessities. He rains down blessings from heaven upon us and causes the earth to bring forth our provision. He gives us our food and clothing, and while we are spending the income of one year, he is preparing the supply for another year. He sweetens our lives with countless comforts and gratifies all our longings with suitable things. The eye of his providence is always upon us, and he watches over our safety when we are in a deep sleep, unaware of him and of ourselves.

In case we think these proofs of his kindness are nothing special because they are the easy efforts of his omnipotent power and do not cause him any trouble or pain, he has taken a more wonderful method of endearing himself to us. He has proved his affection for us by suffering, as well as by doing. And he took on our nature because he could not suffer in his own. The eternal Son of God clothed himself with the weakness of our flesh and left the fellowship of the innocent and blessed spirits who knew how to love and adore him perfectly. He did this so that he might dwell among men, wrestle with the stubborn hearts of this rebellious race to restore their allegiance and joy, and finally to offer himself up as a sacrifice and appeasement of God's wrath for them.

I recall that one of the poets had an ingenious ability to express the passion that overcame him after a long resistance. He said that the God of love shot all his golden arrows at him, but could never pierce his heart until he finally put himself into the bow and fired himself straight into his heart. I believe this gives us a vague impression of God's method of dealing with men. For a long time he contended with a stubborn world and rained down many blessings upon them. And when all his other gifts could not prevail, he finally made a gift of himself to prove his affection and engage theirs.

The account which we have of our Savior's life in the Gospels continually presents us with the story of his love. All the pains that he took and the troubles that he endured were the wonderful effects and unstoppable evidences of it. But oh! That last, that dismal scene! Is it possible to remember it and question his kindness, or deny him ours? Here, here it is, my dear friend, that we should fix our most serious and solemn thoughts, "that Christ may dwell in our hearts by faith, that we being rooted and grounded in love, may be able to comprehend with all saints, what is the breadth, length, depth, and height, and to know the love of Christ which exceeds knowledge, that we may be filled with all the fullness of God."

We should regularly consider the many tokens of favor and love which God has given to each of us. He has put up with our follies and sins for so long, waited to be gracious to us, wrestled with the stubbornness of our hearts, and tested every method to reclaim us. We should keep a mental recording of all the great blessings and deliverances we have experienced. Some of them have been orchestrated in a way that we would clearly perceive that they were not the results of chance, but the gracious works of God's favor, and the answers of our prayers.

We mustn't poison our thoughts of these things with any harsh or unworthy suspicion, as if they were designed on purpose to increase our guilt and eternal damnation. No, no my friend, God is love, and he takes no pleasure in the ruin of his creatures. If they abuse his goodness, turn his grace into license to gratify their senses, and subsequently plunge themselves into a greater depth of guilt and misery, it is the work of their obstinate wickedness, and not the design of the benefits he bestows.

If these considerations have given birth to a real love and affection in our hearts toward Almighty God, it will easily lead us into the other branches of real Christianity. Therefore, I won't have to elaborate on them as much.

To Acquire Charity, We Must Remember That All Men Are Closely Related to God

We shall find our hearts enlarged in charity toward men by considering their relation to God and the imprints of his image that are stamped upon them. They are not only his creatures, the workmanship of his hand, but ones he takes special care of. He has a very dear and tender concern for them. He has laid the plans for their happiness before the foundations of the world, and is willing to live and fellowship with them throughout eternity. The lowest and most despicable person we behold is the offspring of heaven, one of the children of the Most High. And however unworthy of that relation his behavior might be, as long as God has not formally renounced and disowned him by a final sentence, he desires that we acknowledge him as one of his.

Therefore, it is God's desire that we embrace all with a sincere and respectful affection. You know what a great concern we usually have for those that belong to someone we love. How gladly we embrace every opportunity to gratify the child or servant of a friend. We would surely have love for all men spring unforced from our love of God, if we remember the interest he is pleased to have for them. This is increased as we consider that every soul is dearer to him than the entire material world is, and that he did not believe the blood of his Son was too great a price for their redemption.

Men Carry His Image Upon Them

Again, as all men stand in a close relation to God, so they still have so much of his image stamped on them to obligate and motivate us to love them. In some, this image is more obvious and captivating, and we can discern the lovely vestige of wisdom and goodness. And even though in others it is terribly dirtied and defaced, yet is it not altogether destroyed. At least some features still remain. All are given souls that possess the ability to think and that are eternal. All are given reason and wills capable of the highest and most excellent things.

If they are currently disordered and out of tune because of wickedness and folly, this may indeed affect our compassion for them. But it is not a reasonable excuse to extinguish our love for them. When we see a person with a crude nature, a perverse disposition, full of malice and hypocrisy, very foolish and very proud, it is difficult to fall in love with one who appears to be so unpleasant and unattractive. But when we think of these evil qualities as the diseases and disorders of a soul that is capable of all the wisdom and goodness that has adorned the best of saints, and that may one day be raised to such heights of perfection to make it a fit companion for the holy angels, our aversion will turn into pity. And we will view him with the same resentments we would have when we look upon a beautiful body that was mangled with wounds or disfigured by some horrible disease. Regardless of how much we hate the vices, we will not cease to love the man.

To Acquire Purity We Should Consider the Dignity of Our Nature

In the next aspect of real Christianity, for purifying our souls and untangling our affections from the pleasures and enjoyments of this lower life, let us frequently ponder the excellence and dignity of our nature. It is very shameful and unworthy for so noble and divine a creature as the soul of man to sink and become immersed in base and sensual lusts, or to become absorbed with meaningless and excessive pleasures, so that the delight in pleasures that are substantial and spiritual is lost. To live in such a low state is to feed and pamper the animal nature while the man and the Christian in us are starved. If we were mindful of what we are and for what purpose we were made, we would learn to have a proper respect and admiration of ourselves. It would give birth to a holy humility and modesty, and make us very shy and reserved in the use of the most innocent and inoffensive pleasures.

We Should Meditate on the Joys of Heaven Often

Another effective practice for the development of purity is the frequent lifting of our thoughts toward heaven. We should consider the joys that are at God's right hand, "the pleasures that endure for evermore." "For every man that has this hope in him purifies himself even as he is pure." If our heavenly country is frequently in our thoughts, it will make us "strangers and pilgrims abstaining from fleshly lusts that war against the soul." It will help us to keep ourselves "unspotted from this world" so that we may be prepared for the enjoyments and pleasures of the other.

But we must ensure that our notions of heaven are not ignorant and carnal. We must not dream of a Mohammedan paradise, or settle on the metaphors and shadows often used to represent these joys. This could easily have the opposite effect. It might entangle us further in carnal affections, and prepare us to indulge ourselves with excessive foretastes of the pleasures we have placed our everlasting happiness in.

But when we begin to understand the real meaning of these pure and spiritual pleasures, when the happiness we fix our thoughts on comes from the sight, love, and enjoyment of God, and our minds are filled with the hopes and expectations of that blessed state, oh how low and despicable everything here below will appear in our eyes! Then with disdain we will reject the ignorant and polluted pleasures that would deprive us of the celestial enjoyments now, or make us less prepared for eternity, and diminish our desire for what really matters!

Humility Arises From the Contemplation of Our Failures

The last branch of real Christianity is humility. To be sure, we can never lack material for consideration to acquire it. All our wickedness, imperfections, follies, and sins may help to pull down that fond and exaggerated conceit we are likely to entertain about ourselves. The root of the esteem that others may have for us is their knowledge or perception of some little bit of good, combined with their ignorance of a great deal of evil that may be in us. If they were thoroughly acquainted with us, they would quickly change their opinion. If the thoughts that pass in our heart during the best and most serious day of our lives were exposed to public view, they would pronounce us to be either malicious or ridiculous.

Even though we conceal our failings from one another, we are surely conscious of them ourselves. Some serious reflections on them would severely limit and subdue the arrogance of our spirits. In this way holy men have come to really think worse of themselves than of any other person in the world. Not because they knew that the ignorant and scandalous vices in their nature are more heinous than the surprise attacks of temptations and weakness, but because they are far more focused on their own corruptions than on those of their neighbors. They considered all that made their own corruptions more serious, and everything that might be suggested to diminish and alleviate those of others.

Thoughts of God Give Us the Lowest Thoughts of Ourselves

But it is well observed by a pious writer, that the deepest and most pure humility doesn't arise primarily from the consideration of our own faults and defects. It is cultivated by a calm and quiet contemplation of God's purity and goodness. Our spots never appear more vividly than when we place them before this Infinite Light. We never seem less in our own eyes than when we look down upon ourselves from on high. Oh! How little, how nothing all those shadows of perfection that we value ourselves by appear then! The humility that comes from a view of our own sinfulness and misery is more turbulent and boisterous. But the other lays us just as low, lacking nothing but the anguish and vexation of our souls that tend to boil when we are the primary object of our thoughts.

Prayer is Another Instrument of Real Christianity: The Advantages of Internal Prayer

There remains yet another practice for acquiring a holy Christ-like disposition in the soul, fervent and hearty prayer. Holiness is the gift of God, indeed, the greatest gift he bestows or that we are capable of receiving. He has promised his Holy Spirit to those who ask. In prayer we make the closest approach to God and lie open to the influences of heaven. Then it is that the sun of righteousness visits us with his most direct rays, dissipates our darkness, and imprints his image on our souls.

I won't stress the advantages of this exercise or the proper characteristics of prayer at this time. There is no need, due to all of the books that treat this subject. I shall only tell you that there is one aspect of prayer where we make use of the voice that is necessary in public, and may sometimes be advantageous in private. There is another where, although we utter no sound, yet we conceive the expressions and form the words in our minds.

There is a third and more sublime kind of a prayer where the soul takes a higher flight. Having collected all its forces through long and serious meditation, it fires itself like an arrow toward God in sighs, groans, and thoughts too vast for words. Sometimes it occurs after a deep contemplation of the Divine perfections manifested in all his works of wonder. Then the soul addresses itself to him in the profoundest adoration of his majesty and glory. Sometimes after sorrowful reflections on its vileness and mistakes, the soul prostrates itself before him with the greatest confusion and sorrow, not daring to lift up its eyes or utter one word in his presence. At other times, after thorough consideration of the beauty of holiness and the unspeakable joy of those that are truly good, it pants after God and sends up such vigorous and ardent desires as no words can sufficiently express. It continues, repeating each of these nonverbal expressions for as long as it finds itself upheld by the force and impulse of the previous meditation.

This internal prayer is the most effectual kind for purifying the soul and forming it into a holy and religious state. It may be called the great secret of devotion and one of the most powerful instruments of the divine life. Maybe the apostle had a special high regard for it, when he says that "the Spirit helps our weaknesses making intercession for us with groanings that cannot be uttered." Or, the original may be translated, "that cannot be worded."

Even though this kind of prayer is so effectual, I don't recommend that it supersede the use of the other. We have so many individual things to pray for. Every petition of this internal kind of prayer requires so much time and so great a resolve of spirit, that it would be difficult to address them all in this way. And time is not the only constraint. The deep sighs and heaving of the heart that accompany it are by nature draining, and make it hard to continue very long. Yet there is no doubt that a few of these inward aspirations will do more than a vast number of fluent and tender expressions.

Real Christianity is Advanced by the Same Resource That Started It: The Practice of the Lord's Supper

Thus, my dear friend, I have briefly proposed the method that I believe to be proper for molding the soul into a holy state. The same activities that serve to acquire this divine nature must always be practiced for strengthening and advancing it. Therefore, I will recommend one more for that purpose. It is the frequent and conscientious participation in the Lord's Supper.

The Lord's Supper is distinctively appointed to nourish and grow the spiritual life after it has been birthed in the soul. All the aspects of real Christianity come together in this ordinance. As we participate, we put into practice all of the spiritual disciplines we have examined. It is then that we make the most critical survey of our actions and place the strictest obligations on ourselves. This is where are our minds are raised to the highest contempt toward the things of this world, and every grace exercises itself with the greatest activity and vigor. All the subjects of spiritual contemplation present themselves to us with the greatest advantage here. If ever the soul makes its most powerful sallies toward heaven, and assaults it with a holy and acceptable force, it is here. And certainly the neglect or careless performance of this duty is one of the primary causes of spiritual immaturity, making us remain spiritual babies.

But it is time to close this letter that has grown to a far greater bulk than intended. If these poor papers can do you the smallest service, I will consider myself very happy in this undertaking. At least I am hopeful you will kindly accept the sincere endeavors of a person who would attempt to acquit himself of part of the debt owed to you.

A Prayer

"And now, O most gracious God, father and fountain of mercy and goodness, you have blessed us with the knowledge of our happiness and the way that leads to it. Excite in our souls fervent desires after that knowledge to the extent that we may be diligent in the way that leads to it. Let us not trust in our own strength, nor distrust your divine assistance. Even when we are giving our best effort, teach us to always depend on you for success. Open our eyes, O God, and teach us out of your law. Bless us with an exact and tender sense of our duty and with the knowledge to discern perverse things. Oh! That our ways were directed to keep your statutes, and then we will not be ashamed, for we have respect for all your commandments.

"Control our hearts with a generous and holy disdain for all the poor enjoyments which this world offers to entice us. Then they will never be able to entice our affections or betray us to any sin. Turn away our eyes from beholding vanity, and breathe life in us in your law. Fill our souls with such a deep awareness and full persuasion of the great truths that you have revealed in the Bible. Then they will influence and regulate our whole behavior, and then the life we live from now on in the flesh we may live through faith in the Son of God.

"Oh! We ask that the infinite perfections of your blessed character and the awe inspiring expressions of your goodness and love conquer and overpower our hearts. As we meditate on your attributes and works, cause our hearts to be constantly rising toward you ablaze with the most devout affections. In your light, cause our hearts to be enlarged in sincere and cordial love toward all mankind for your sake. Win our hearts so that we may cleanse ourselves from all filthiness of flesh and spirit, perfecting holiness in your fear, without which we can never hope to behold and enjoy you.

"Finally, O God, grant that the contemplation of what you are and of what we are, may each humble and prostrate us before you. Grant that it also stir in us the strongest and most ardent aspirations toward you. We desire to cease striving against and to surrender ourselves to the direction of the Holy Spirit, so lead us in your truth and teach us, for you are the God of our salvation. Guide us with your counsel and then receive us into glory because of the grace and intercession of your blessed Son our Savior." Amen

-Notes-

-Notes-

Made in the USA
Monee, IL
03 January 2025

75842900R00080